I0540425

UNDERSTANDING CRICKET

A GUIDE FOR AMERICANS

BY HIRSH LEFF

Table of Contents

Foreword

Why Cricket Deserves a Spot in the American Heart

Cricket is experiencing an unprecedented surge in popularity across the United States. Just three years ago, I knew nothing about the game, but today I have come to deeply appreciate its greatness. When I first searched for information, I found plenty of resources, but most were unhelpful for Americans like me, who had been raised to perceive cricket as a pompous British pastime that dragged on for weeks.

While cricket is quintessentially British, it has unexpected ties to early American history. George Washington reportedly played the game with his troops at Valley Forge, and Benjamin Franklin brought the 1744 Laws—the official rulebook of cricket—to America from London. As late as 1859, Abraham Lincoln attended a cricket match. Interestingly, the Founding Fathers borrowed the term "President" from cricket club leaders, finding it far less regal than proposed titles like "His Highness."

Surprisingly, cricket predates baseball in America. The belief that Abner Doubleday invented baseball is a myth; he never claimed to have created the game. In fact, Jane Austen mentioned "base-ball" as early as 1799, two decades before Doubleday was even born. Cricket and baseball share more than just history; baseball adopted several terms from cricket, including knuckleball, caught out, innings, umpires, and runs. Even the beloved "hat trick," now a staple of hockey, originated in cricket when fans chipped in to buy a bowler a new hat after he took three consecutive wickets.

UNDERSTANDING CRICKET

The first international match in sports history was a cricket game between the U.S. and Canada in 1844. This inaugural Auty Cup match took place in Manhattan and attracted a crowd of 5,000 fans. Remarkably, the Auty Cup continues to this day, showcasing the enduring connection between our two nations. However, despite its early prominence, cricket lost popularity during the Civil War, as baseball required less space and equipment.

If cricket seems complicated, it's likely because you're comparing it to a sport you've known since childhood. In reality, cricket is simpler and more intuitive than baseball, making it easier for kids and newcomers to learn and enjoy. I once took a Croatian friend to a baseball game, and after three hours of my explanations, he was more baffled than when we started. Have you ever tried to explain the infield fly rule or the dropped third strike? It's enough to confuse anyone!

Cricket is experiencing an extraordinary resurgence in the U.S., now home to over three million fans and recognized as the fastest-growing market for the sport worldwide. This rapid growth has been fueled by substantial investments, including the launch of major and minor franchise leagues. In 2024, the U.S. proudly hosted 20 thrilling matches of the T20 World Cup across Dallas, New York, and Florida. Looking ahead, cricket's momentum will continue with its return to the Olympics in 2028, where the American team will compete on home soil in Los Angeles as the host nation.

This book starts with my personal journey and explains why I fell in love with this incredible sport. Chapter One serves as a crash course, providing you with enough knowledge to watch and enjoy your first match. Whether you develop a passion for cricket like I did or discover that it's not for you, I commend you for giving it a try!

In the following chapters, we will explore where to watch a game and what to focus on before delving into cricket's key elements: batting, bowling, and fielding. We will also discuss different formats of the game, the growing prominence of women in cricket, and other fundamental concepts to deepen your understanding of the sport.

Please note that while cricket has several formats, I will focus on **T20** cricket, which is designed to attract newer and younger fans. T20 matches last about three hours, feature high scores, and provide a fast-paced experience. Launched in 2023, Major League Cricket is now introducing T20 to audiences across the U.S. with teams representing major American cities. In a future chapter, I will explain the other major formats, such as ODI and Test, but T20 remains the most popular format globally and is poised to dominate in the United States.

This is the book I wish I had when I first discovered cricket. It's designed to get you watching and enjoying matches within an hour, providing just enough knowledge to make you a confident fan—without overwhelming you with historical trivia or unnecessary minutia. With time, your understanding and appreciation of the sport will grow, as will your enjoyment. Cricket has brought me immense joy, and I can't wait for you to experience its thrills, strategies, and unforgettable moments. Let's dive in!

Cricket's Edge: What Sets It Apart

Cricket Always Has a Winner High-scoring and decisive, cricket matches avoid the frustration of 1-1 ties often seen in soccer and hockey. In timed formats, ties are impossible, ensuring every game has a definitive conclusion.

A Game of Dramatic Twists A single over can completely change the course of a match. Upsets are common, making every game exciting. The U.S.'s overtime victory against Pakistan at the 2024 T20 Cricket World Cup shocked the world and showcased cricket's unpredictability.

Constant Action Cricket features minimal downtime, ensuring a brisk and engaging pace. There is always something happening on the field, keeping both players and spectators continuously involved throughout the game.

Year-Round Excitement Cricket never takes a break! While baseball's 180-day season may feel endless, cricket leagues and tournaments last just 3 to 6 weeks, with events held throughout the year. Summer in the U.S. brings local cricket, and during winter, we enjoy matches from Australia's sweltering summer. There's even an iconic competition every December 26th.

Global Rivalries Over Franchise Feuds Forget waiting for the Olympics—nations clash in cricket multiple times a year. Rivalries such as Australia vs. England and India vs. Pakistan bring unmatched passion and drama that franchise leagues cannot replicate. Whenever an American team competes against another country, it becomes a major event, generating excitement and fostering national pride as the U.S. establishes itself in the global cricket community.

Simultaneous Offense and Defense Unlike sports where teams take turns on offense and defense, cricket players juggle both at once. Batting, bowling, and fielding require intricate tactics and real-time adjustments, all led by the on-field captain—not a manager on the sidelines.

Exceptional Athleticism Cricketers are among the most versatile athletes in the world. Batters often spend over an hour at the crease, showcasing their focus and endurance. Each player is expected to excel in fielding while also specializing in batting, bowling, or both. This unique combination of skills and adaptability distinguishes cricket from other sports.

The Right Call, Every Time Cricket's review system ensures accurate decisions, supported by entertaining technology. Umpires rarely make mistakes, eliminating the need to argue with officials. Players and captains respect decisions instead of questioning them.

Inclusive and Welcoming Cricket has made significant strides in promoting diversity, with women's cricket now a major and celebrated aspect of the sport. Supported at both domestic and international levels, women's leagues and tournaments showcase incredible talent and enhance cricket's global appeal.

Fast, Fun, and Flexible Cricket strikes the perfect balance between action and downtime. There's plenty of scoring, but also enough breaks to multitask, catch up with the world, or even join halfway through a match without missing out.

Family-Friendly and Accessible Cricket promotes a positive atmosphere free from fights or heated disagreements. In the U.S., games are either affordable or free, making the sport an ideal choice for the entire family.

Cricket Combines the Best of Other Sports Imagine baseball but better! Cricket offers home runs, aggressive running, strategic duels, athletic fielding, extra innings, and high-stakes playoff series—all in one game.

Data Galore for Stats Lovers Cricket's endless statistics keep fans engaged. Predict the final score using run rates or compare today's stars with legends of the past—there's always a number to crunch.

A Sport That's Growing and Evolving While Test cricket boasts a 150-year legacy, T20 cricket is a modern format introduced in 2003. With new teams forming yearly and records constantly being shattered, cricket is in an exciting era of transformation.

Respect and Camaraderie Cricketers play with integrity. There's no "unwritten code" like baseball's retaliation pitches, and the game is governed by established laws that emphasize respect and propriety.

One Name, One Sport Cricket doesn't suffer from name confusion like soccer/football. Around a quarter of the world shares the same passion for this incredible sport.

Introduction

How Cricket Became My American Pastime

As a semi-retired empty nester, I found myself searching for a new hobby to fill my days. Sports had once been a great passion of mine, but now it was just me, my wonderful wife, and our Border Collie, Moxie, sharing a quieter life. Although I enjoy scuba diving and flying drones, these activities still left me with plenty of free time. I craved something new—something that could challenge my mind and spark fresh excitement.

Growing up in New England, I followed professional sports teams and the Olympics. Thirty years later, after relocating to Raleigh, North Carolina—the college sports capital of the nation—I found no reason to support a college team from a school I hadn't attended. Only March Madness captured my attention.

Having been a fan of baseball and hockey for years I still enjoyed attending games, but had lost interest in watching them on TV. You may disagree but to me baseball games seem to drag on endlessly, and the season felt like it went on forever. Hockey, while thrilling in person, was frustrating to follow on TV—even in high definition.

I remain a devoted fan of my Pittsburgh Steelers and Boston Celtics, watching as many games as possible. However, my interest in football and basketball diminishes when my teams are not playing. This prompted me to question how much I truly love these sports if I can only watch my favorite teams. While NFL ratings may be enormous, how much of that is driven by betting?

Some sports never captured my attention. Pro wrestling and MMA don't appeal to me. As for soccer, I can't imagine dedicating 90+ minutes to a game that ends in a 0-0 tie. The lack of stats and the mystery of stoppage time make it unappealing. Boxing, once a giant in the sports world, is now a shadow of its former self.

UNDERSTANDING CRICKET

Cricket had been a faint presence on my radar for some time. Years ago, I heard Sir Stephen Fry—an actor, author, and renowned polymath whose intellect and wit I deeply admire—singing the praises of the sport. He spoke of its timeless elegance, strategic depth, and intellectual appeal, and his words lingered in my mind. However, my first attempt to watch cricket during a trip to St. Kitts left me thoroughly bewildered. Unsure where to begin, I decided to shelve the idea for another time.

Everything changed when my wife and I downsized to a townhome in Cary, North Carolina. Never cutting grass again was reason enough to celebrate, but the vibrant South Asian community in nearby Morrisville introduced me to an unexpected discovery: cricket. The town built a beautiful cricket field, and when I saw a schedule for the Morrisville Raptors—a local minor league team—I decided to check out a game.

Church Street Park: Smaran Nagaraj, CC BY-SA 4.0
<https://creativecommons.org/licenses/by-sa/4.0>, via Wikimedia Commons

One Friday night, I arrived at the cricket field with no expectations and found myself immersed in a three-hour match, surrounded by families in a lively, welcoming park with free admission. Although I didn't grasp much of what was happening, the game piqued my curiosity and left me with a notebook full of questions. Over the next 24 hours, I dove headfirst into YouTube and scoured the internet, and gradually, the sport began to make sense.

The first thing I learned was the basics: batters score runs and can be out in various ways. Each bowler delivers six balls per "over," with a total of 20 overs (120 balls) in an innings. And yes, it's "innings," not "inning"—cricket is quirky that way. One team bats first, aiming to score as many runs as possible in this first innings, while the second team bats in the second innings, needing to surpass the first team's score by at least one run to win. As I began to grasp these concepts, the charm of the game revealed itself, and I became completely hooked.

I also discovered cricket's massive global reach. With 2.5 billion fans, cricket is second only to soccer in popularity worldwide. To my surprise, field hockey ranks third with 2 billion fans, followed by tennis, volleyball, and table tennis. Baseball and basketball? Both trail behind, with 500 million and 400 million fans, respectively.

Armed with this new knowledge, I returned to the field for the second game on Saturday night. I was fortunate to sit near a friendly spectator who patiently answered my endless questions. Each game brought new revelations: Why do fielders keep moving? What happens if the ball gets by the wicketkeeper and rolls into the field? What if the score is tied after both innings are complete?

After the minor league season ended, I began watching cricket on TV through Willow, a streaming service that offers a large library of matches at a reasonable price. The commentators were entertaining, though their jargon often sent me running to Google. Cricket's vocabulary is both fascinating and intimidating, but I quickly learned to distinguish the essential terms from the arcane.

UNDERSTANDING CRICKET

As the short minor league season ended, I realized I needed a team to follow. Cricket's domestic leagues are exciting but brief, with players often competing in multiple leagues each year. I wanted a national team—one that consistently played together.

I chose to follow the England Women's National Cricket Team. My decision wasn't the result of extensive research; I found it manageable to learn the players' names, and it felt fitting to back a team from the birthplace of cricket. Supporting a women's team also aligned with my values, especially during the Caitlin Clark era, which has drawn renewed attention to women's sports. While the team operates as a cohesive unit for most of the year, the players also compete in franchise leagues, where teammates often become rivals.

In 2024, cricket's T20 World Cup was co-hosted by the U.S. and West Indies, and the U.S. stunned the world by defeating Pakistan in a historic upset. The match was even compared to the Miracle on Ice and made headlines globally. For the first time, cricket caught the attention of mainstream American sports media, including my favorite show, *Pardon the Interruption*.

Over the past three years, cricket has become my passion. Americans will love this sport if they give it a chance. You don't need to memorize every rule or know every player. Cricket is a game of challenges, strategy, and joy at every level.

If you're new to cricket, don't worry—there's no need to feel intimidated. Chapter One will provide you with all the essentials to enjoy a match, without overwhelming you with unnecessary details. The rest of the book delves deeper into the game's nuances and includes a handy glossary for quick reference. Cricket fans are famously friendly and love to share their passion, so don't hesitate to strike up a conversation at a game. They'll often be surprised and delighted to see an American taking an interest in their sport. Before long, you'll find yourself becoming part of the community.

I hope cricket brings you as much excitement and fulfillment as it has brought me.

Chapter One

The Essentials: A Crash Course in Cricket

Imagine a baseball game: nine players on the fielding side—a pitcher, a catcher, four infielders, and three outfielders—are focused on preventing the batter at the plate from scoring runs. Each team alternates between fielding and batting, striving to outscore the opponent. The height of both excitement and disappointment occurs with a home run, when the batter hits the ball out of the playing field. The pitcher and batter engage in a strategic duel, while the catcher secures the ball and prepares for the next play. Fielders, guided by strategy and scouting reports, adjust their positions to catch fly balls or tag runners out. Runners, in turn, slide into bases on close plays to avoid being tagged out, as each out is precious. The game concludes when one team records all the necessary outs while holding at least a one-run lead.

Now you're ready for cricket!

In cricket, each team consists of eleven players, with a twelfth player available as a substitute fielder for injured players (though not as a batter or bowler). As before the days of baseball's Designated Hitter Rule, all eleven players are part of the batting lineup. On the fielding side, the **bowler delivers** the ball, while the **wicketkeeper**—similar to a baseball catcher—stands behind the batter to catch the ball or prevent it from getting passed them for extra runs. The remaining nine fielders are strategically positioned across the infield and outfield to prevent runs and take catches. While every player is expected to excel at fielding, most specialize as either bowlers or batters. A select few who excel at both are known as **all-rounders**, prized for their versatility and value to the team.

Cricket Fields: A Unique Playing Space

Cricket is played on fields that are typically oval or round, allowing for play to span a full 360 degrees around the batter. Similar to baseball, the overall field dimensions follow loose guidelines regarding shape and size. However, like baseball's diamond, the infield is precisely defined. At the center of the field is the 22-yard rectangular **Pitch**, groomed as meticulously as a golf putting green. This pitch connects the bowler and the wicketkeeper. Surrounding the pitch is the 30-yard **Circle**, which marks the boundary of the infield.

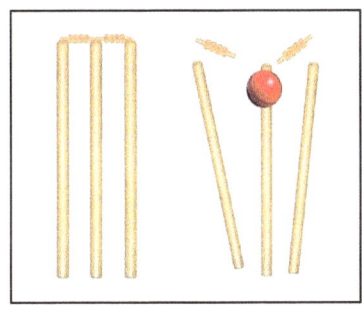

Directly behind the batters, on either side of the pitch, stand three closely spaced poles, each 28 inches tall, known as the **Stumps**. Resting atop them are two small cylindrical pieces of wood called **Bails**. Together, the stumps and bails form what is known as the **Wicket**.

Dismissals (outs) occur when the bails are dislodged from the stumps, rather than by tagging a runner or touching a base as in baseball. The ball can strike the wicket directly, or a fielder with the ball can hit the stumps and knock off the bails.

To achieve a dismissal, at least one bail must be dislodged from its stump. This occurs when the ball passes the batter and strikes the wicket directly. Additionally, the wicketkeeper can dismiss the batter by knocking off the bails while the batters are running **between the wickets** and have not yet reached the safety zone known as the **popping crease.** On some fields, the stumps and bails are fitted with embedded red lights that flash upon dislodgement, creating an exciting and visually dramatic moment for spectators.

A note of caution: the term **Wicket** has several meanings. In this book, wicket will refer either to the combination of stumps and bails or to cricket's equivalent of a baseball out. In other contexts, you may hear wicket used to describe the pitch itself.

The Bowler: Delivering the Magic

The bowler's role is to limit the batting team's runs while attempting to dismiss the batter and **take a wicket**. In this context, the term **wicket** has a second major meaning: it is equivalent to an **out**.

One of the most striking differences between a bowler and a baseball pitcher is their delivery technique. Unlike pitchers, who throw the ball from a stationary position, bowlers use a run-up to generate added momentum and power before releasing the ball. Bowlers must keep their elbow straight during the delivery, which creates a unique motion. Although this style of bowling may seem unconventional at first, it is highly effective, with elite bowlers reaching speeds of 90 to 100 mph.

In baseball, pitchers are classified based on their roles in the game, such as starters or relievers. In contrast, bowlers are categorized by their bowling styles; some focus on sheer speed, while others master the art of spin to deceive batters. Exceptional bowlers are highly valued for their ability to achieve remarkable feats with the ball and change the course of a match. While any player is eligible to bowl, each team has several players who excel at this skill.

At the start of the game, the opening bowler begins their run-up and, upon reaching the marked delivery point, releases the ball with a straight arm. The ball typically bounces once on the pitch before reaching the batter, who may attempt to hit it, let it go, or swing and miss. This delivery marks the first ball of the **over**, a defined segment of the game during which the bowler delivers six legal balls from one end of the pitch. Each over represents a focused phase of play, providing tactical opportunities for both the batting and fielding teams. Once the over is complete, the bowler transitions to a fielding position, and a new bowler takes over from the opposite end of the pitch to deliver the next over.

Each bowler is unique, controlling the speed of their delivery and the area where the ball bounces on the pitch, which determines its height when it reaches the batter. **Fast bowlers** are known for their speed, while **swing bowlers** make the ball move in the air from left to right or vice versa. **Spin bowlers** sacrifice some delivery speed but make the ball to veer left or right after bouncing, making it difficult for the batter to predict its trajectory.

Occasionally, bowlers make errors, such as delivering the ball out of the reach of the batter, comparable to a "ball" call in baseball. The umpire will call a **wide**, penalizing the bowling team by one run and requiring the bowler to make an additional delivery. Bowlers may also mistakenly step over the **front foot line**, resulting in a **no-ball**, which incurs both a **penalty run** and a **free ball**. During a free ball delivery, the batter can take a big swing, as they cannot be caught or bowled out.

Batting: The Art of Scoring Runs

In chess, moves can be offensive, defensive, or strategic, positioning pieces for future tactics. Both players strive to secure a superior position to win while also protecting key pieces that could lead to a quick elimination. Keep this in mind while observing cricket batters.

The primary responsibility of the batter is to **defend the wicket**. If the bowler delivers the ball and the batter fails to hit it, allowing the ball to strike the stumps and dislodge the bails, the batter is dismissed and must leave the field. This brings disappointment to their team and fans alike. This may occur on the very first ball faced or after scoring an impressive 50 runs. You're likely to witness both scenarios within your first few games.

If the batter feels they cannot hit the ball cleanly to score runs, their priority shifts to preventing the ball from hitting the wicket. In such cases, they execute a **defensive shot**, directing the ball into the ground, similar to a bunt in baseball. Although this action does not produce runs, it helps them remain in the game. Conversely, if the ball is not threatening the wicket, the batter may choose to let it pass without attempting a shot. A legal delivery that results in no runs scored is referred to as a **dot ball**.

The batter's secondary responsibility is to score runs. Unlike baseball, there are no strikes or foul balls, allowing the batter to hit in any direction: straight, left, right, or even behind. Any area of the field is fair game for a batter. The batter checks the positioning of the fielders and aims for the gaps.

Fielding: Precision and Agility

Wicketkeeper

Behind the batter stands the cricket equivalent of a baseball catcher, known as the **Keeper** or **Wicketkeeper**. Instantly recognizable, the Keeper is the only fielder wearing gloves—oversized and heavily padded for protection. While these gloves may appear almost comical, they are essential for catching fast-moving balls that slip past or are deflected, or **edged**, by the bat.

In addition to the Keeper and Bowler, the fielding team consists of nine other players. Unlike the Keeper, all fielders must catch the ball barehanded, even though cricket balls are significantly harder and heavier than baseballs. Imagine how different baseball would be if only the catcher had a glove!

Fielding positions are meticulously planned, with the captain orchestrating the setup in real time, responding to the game's progress. These adjustments ensure the team is well-positioned to balance defense and aggression.

To truly appreciate the athleticism of cricketers, envision a fielder diving to catch a ball traveling at 80 mph, securing it barehanded, and then springing to their feet to deliver a precise throw—all in one seamless motion. It's no surprise that many players leave the field with sore hands and a sense of well-earned accomplishment.

Game Flow: How Matches Unfold

The flow of a cricket match is relatively straightforward once the fundamentals are understood. Like football, the game begins with a coin toss between the two captains. The winning captain decides whether their team will bat or field first, a decision influenced by various strategic considerations. Bowling first allows the fielding side to know the **target score** they need to chase when it's their turn to bat. However, several factors influence this choice, including weather conditions, sunlight intensity, batting visibility, and changes in the pitch's pace due to wear or weather. The losing captain then determines which end of the field the opening bowler will start from.

In baseball, each game consists of nine innings, with teams alternating between batting and fielding. This results in 18 changes of sides, each accompanied by commercial breaks lasting about 2 to 3 minutes. Additionally, when a new pitcher enters the game, further delays occur as they complete warm-up throws on the mound, adding another 2 to 3 minutes per change. These frequent pauses, along with breaks between innings, contribute to over an hour of inactivity during the game, where little to no action takes place.

Cricket, in contrast, features only two **innings**. A charming quirk of the game is that the term "innings" is used for both singular and plural—perhaps for the same whimsical reason that the British say "maths" instead of "math." In each match, one team bats for the entirety of the first innings, while the other bats during the second innings, with teams switching between batting and fielding only once.

Each innings is divided into **overs**, with one bowler delivering six consecutive legal balls in each over. Once an over is completed, a new bowler takes the ball and delivers the next six balls from the opposite end of the field. In T20 cricket, an innings consists of 20 overs, totaling 120 legal deliveries per innings, with two innings making up the game. Each bowler is limited to a maximum of four overs per match, promoting strategic use of the bowling lineup and preventing any single bowler from dominating the game.

A team continues batting until one of the following four conditions is met:

1. The team has faced all **20 overs** (a total of 120 legal deliveries).
2. **Ten batters are dismissed**, resulting in the loss of ten wickets, leaving no players remaining to bat.
3. The game is interrupted by **weather conditions**, such as rain, which halts play.
4. In the **second innings**, the batting team successfully outscores their opponent, thereby concluding the match.

Once the first innings concludes, the roles reverse. The team that fielded now bats, aiming to surpass the first team's score by at least one run. They must achieve this **target score** before running out of balls or batters. This single-role switch streamlines the game by reducing unnecessary interruptions and keeping the focus on the importance of each delivery. Early outs are highly valuable, as the top of the batting lineup features dangerous batters, creating anticipation with each ball bowled. The climax intensifies as the team batting in the second innings approaches its target, requiring both sides to balance risk and reward.

Cricket's **Powerplay** introduces an additional strategic dimension to the game. During the first six overs, known as the **Powerplay Overs**, teams are limited to only two fielders in the outfield beyond the 30-yard circle, which marks the boundary of the infield area surrounding the pitch. This restriction gives batters a clear advantage and encourages aggressive batting in the early innings. Once the Powerplay concludes, up to five fielders can be positioned outside the circle, shifting the balance of power back toward the bowlers and fielders for the remainder of the innings (overs 7-20).

If both teams are tied after their innings, a Super Over decides the winner. Each team gets an additional over (six balls) and selects their top bowler and batter to compete. If the score remains tied after the Super Over, additional Super Overs are played until a winner emerges, ensuring a decisive outcome.

Weather plays a pivotal role in cricket, as rain can disrupt or even cancel matches. To address this, cricket employs the Duckworth–Lewis–Stern (DLS) method, a mathematical formula used to fairly determine the winner of rain-affected games. While the method is a bit complex at first, don't worry about fully understanding it just yet—it will make more sense when you encounter it during a game.

Scoring: The Basics Explained

One of the biggest challenges for newcomers to cricket is adjusting to the sight of two batters on the field at the same time. This setup will seem strange and awkward to those familiar with baseball. However, with a little time, you'll come to appreciate the added layers of complexity and strategy it brings to the game. Just remember that although there are two batters on the field, only one is the active batter at any given time.

To clarify this concept, consider a baseball analogy: One batter stands at home plate while another is positioned at first base. When the batter hits the ball, both players run toward and then past each other, switching places and tagging their new "bases" for safety. Once they both successfully reach their new positions, one run is scored. Instead of stopping at one run, they could return to their original spots for a second run—provided they have enough time and confidence to avoid being tagged out. If the ball reaches the plate before they do, they're out.

Now, take this concept and reposition "first base" to the pitcher's mound, so the runners travel back and forth between the pitcher and the catcher. This, in essence, is how cricket works.

UNDERSTANDING CRICKET

In cricket, there are always two batters on the field. The **Striker** is the active batter positioned in front of the wicket at the wicketkeeper's end, while the **Non-striker** stands at the opposite wicket near the bowler. After the Striker hits the ball, both batters run to the opposite wickets, carrying their bats. Once the play concludes, whichever batter is at the wicketkeeper's end for the next ball will be the striker.

When facing a ball traveling at speeds exceeding 90 mph and altering its trajectory mid-flight, the Striker must make an almost instantaneous decision among three options:

- **Attempt to hit the ball**: The Striker aims to score runs by either placing the ball in a gap or hitting a boundary.

- **Play a defensive ground shot**: With a controlled stroke, the batter directs the ball into the ground to protect the wicket.

- **Leave the ball**: Judging that the ball will not hit the stumps, the Striker allows it to pass untouched, conserving energy and reducing risk.

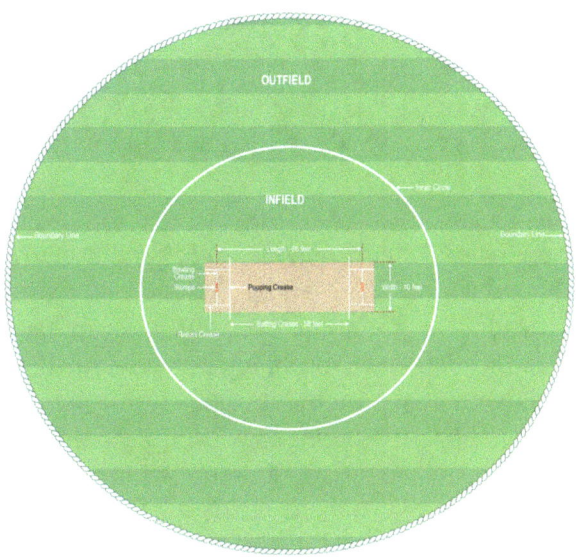

Batters can score runs by running between the wickets, earning one run for each complete trip. When the ball is hit into play, fielders must retrieve it and return it to either the bowler or the wicketkeeper, at which point play stops. If the ball is fielded by a nearby player, the batters may opt to remain stationary to avoid the risk of being run out. However, when the ball is struck into the outfield, there is often enough time for the batters to run between the wickets and ground their bat or foot past the crease to secure a run. Quick and aggressive runners may even complete a second or third run before the fielding team retrieves the ball. While it is technically possible to score four or more runs by running alone, the majority of runs are scored in singles, twos, or threes.

At the edge of the field lies the **boundary marker**, which separates the playing area from the non-playing area. Traditionally marked by a rope, the boundary has evolved to include other forms, such as painted lines or fencing. Think of it as the "wall" in baseball. When a batter strikes the ball over the boundary without it touching the ground, it earns **six runs**, a moment of triumph celebrated as a **Six**. Conversely, if the ball first bounces within the field of play before hitting or crossing the boundary, it scores **four runs**, commonly referred to as a **Boundary**.

In cricket, unlike baseball, batters stop running as soon as a **Boundary** or a **Six** is confirmed. There's no celebratory lap around the field to overshadow the opposing team. Instead, batters exchange a quick fist bump or high five in the middle of the pitch, offering a modest acknowledgment of their achievement before returning to their positions.

Wickets: How Batters Get Out

Batters remain **at the crease** until they are dismissed, a process known as **losing a wicket**. A dismissal can happen on the very first ball a batter faces, or they may remain at the crease for the entire innings. All eleven players in the team are eligible to bat, with the strongest batters typically positioned at the top or middle of the lineup. However, since two batters must always be on the field, an innings concludes when the team loses its tenth wicket.

Another unique feature of cricket is that umpires don't make dismissal calls without prompting. The fielding team must **appeal** to the umpire when they believe a batter is out, typically by shouting **"How's that?"** or **"Howzat!"** The umpire then signals whether the batter is **Out** or **Not Out**. If the fielding team doesn't appeal—even when the batter should clearly be out—the game continues as if nothing happened.

In baseball, batters can be caught, struck out, grounded out, or tagged out. In cricket, there are ten ways for a batter to be dismissed, but the following are the ones you are most likely to encounter:

- **Caught Out**: Similar to a fly ball in baseball, if the batter hits the ball into the air and it is caught by a fielder before touching the ground, the batter is dismissed and must leave the field.

- **Bowled Out**: The batter's primary responsibility is to protect the stumps behind them. If the bowler delivers a ball that bypasses both the bat and the batter, striking the stumps and dislodging the bails, the batter is considered **Bowled Out**.

- **Leg Before Wicket (LBW)**: During play, balls often strike the batter's leg pads. If the ball hits the pads without touching the bat, and the umpire determines that it would have gone on to hit the stumps had the batter not obstructed it, the batter is declared out. Due to the complexity of this decision, which requires an assessment of the ball's trajectory, it is often referred to the third umpire for video review. Advanced technologies such as **UltraEdge®** and **Ball Tracking** are used to ensure accuracy in these calls.

- **Caught Behind**: If the batter edges (nicks) the ball—similar to a foul ball in baseball—and it is caught mid-air by the wicketkeeper or a close fielder before touching the ground, the batter is dismissed. This type of dismissal is why multiple fielders, often referred to as the **slip cordon**, are strategically positioned near the batter to capitalize on these opportunities.

- **Run Out**: The area surrounding the stumps is marked by lines known as the **crease**, which define the batter's safe zone. While running between the wickets, a batter risks being run out if neither their bat nor any part of their body is grounded within the crease. A run out occurs when a fielder successfully breaks the stumps with the ball before the batter can return to the safety of the crease.

- **Stumped**: Similar to a pick-off in baseball, this dismissal happens when the batter steps out of the crease to attempt a shot. If the wicketkeeper collects the ball and breaks the stumps while the batter is outside the crease, the batter is **stumped** and dismissed.

- **Hit Wicket**: A batter is dismissed as **Hit Wicket** if they accidentally dislodge the bails by striking the stumps with their bat or body the ball is in play.

During a match, either team may occasionally disagree with an on-field umpire's decision. Instead of displaying hostility, they can use one of their allotted appeals to request a review by the "third umpire." This umpire, typically seated in air-conditioned comfort with an elevated view of the field, utilizes the **Decision Review System (DRS)®** to reassess the call. Similar to Hawk-Eye® in tennis, DRS employs advanced technology to confirm or overturn the on-field umpire's decision with greater accuracy.

The most common appeal is the **Leg Before Wicket (LBW)** decision. Once the captain decides to appeal a call the review process begins with the third umpire verifying whether the bowler's foot landed legally behind the **front foot line** at the time of delivery.

Next, the **UltraEdge®** system—microphones positioned near the stumps which captures audio signals to determine if the ball made contact with the bat or pads. This technology displays sound waves on a screen, synchronized with slow-motion replays. If the ball is close to the bat and the video evidence is inconclusive, UltraEdge becomes the decisive tool. If a sharp spike on the graph at the moment of potential contact confirms that the ball touched the bat, the third umpire overturns the LBW decision and declares the batter **Not Out,** as contact with the bat nullifies the LBW appeal.

If the delivery is deemed legal and it is confirmed that the ball touched the leg pad but did not touch the bat, the review proceeds to **Ball Tracking**. This stage utilizes **Virtual Eye®** technology to analyze the ball's recorded trajectory up to the point of impact with the pads, predicting its path as if the batter's leg had not obstructed it. An onscreen graphic indicates whether the ball would have hit the stumps, missed over the top, or veered to the side. The batter is declared out only if the projection conclusively shows that the ball would have struck the stumps.

The third umpire announces instructions to the on-field umpire via an open microphone, advising whether to uphold or change the original call. If there is insufficient evidence to make a final determination, they will instruct the umpire to **Stick With** their original decision, and the team retains their challenge.

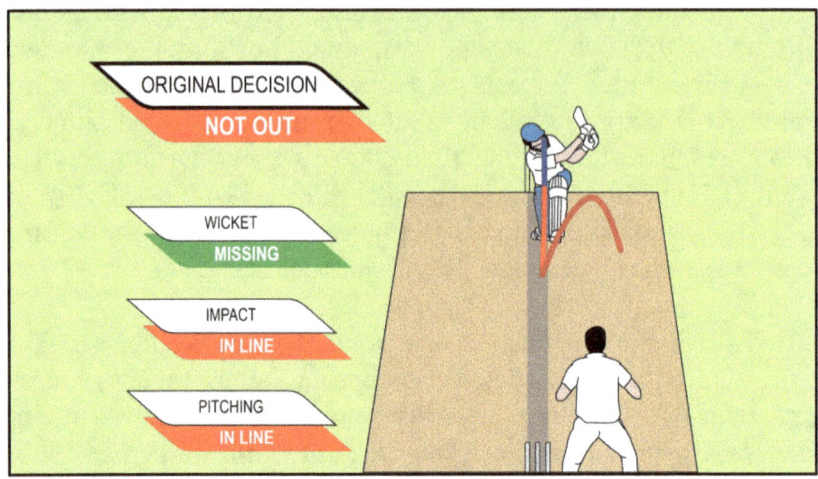

Duckworth-Lewis-Stern: Cricket's Rain Rule

Weather is the eternal adversary of cricket. It is the umpires' responsibility to manage rain delays, which halt the game until the rain stops and the field conditions are deemed safe. No one wants to see a player injured due to slippery ground.

Rain can delay the start of a game, leaving insufficient time for a full match. In such cases, the number of overs for both teams may be reduced, leading to shorter innings. Batters often adopt an aggressive approach to maximize runs within the limited time, while bowlers strive to capitalize on mistakes made under the pressure of these altered conditions. Although brief, these condensed games often produce thrilling finishes and highlight the fast-paced, high-stakes nature of cricket when time is of the essence.

Some matches cannot resume once rain sets in. If each team has not faced at least five overs, the game is declared a **No Result**, with no winner. However, if both teams have completed at least five overs, the outcome is determined using an algorithm known as the **Duckworth-Lewis-Stern (DLS)** method.

The DLS method calculates the percentage of resources—overs and wickets—remaining for both teams at the point of interruption. It then determines a **Par Score** for the team batting second, which represents the target they need to win. This Par Score updates dynamically after each ball as the remaining resources are consumed.

If rain **interrupts play** and the match is called off, the umpires use the DLS calculation to determine the winner. For example, if the batting team's par score is 95 and they have scored 97 runs when play is stopped, they win. Conversely, if they have only scored 92 runs, they lose.

During broadcasts, the par score is often displayed on-screen to keep viewers informed as rain approaches. Each additional run helps reduce the gap with the par score, while **dot balls** and wickets influence the par score by reducing the remaining resources. Wickets, in particular, are heavily weighted in the DLS calculation and significantly impact the batting team's projected chances.

The beauty of this system lies in its ability to maintain excitement, even in rain-affected games. The DLS method ensures that every ball bowled and every run scored contributes meaningfully to the final result, creating the thrill of a run chase even in abbreviated matches.

Interpreting the Score Graphics

Cricket scoreboards differ in presentation across TV broadcasts and digital platforms, yet they all aim to convey essential information about the game's progress. This subchapter breaks down the elements of a cricket scoreboard, offering a clear understanding of how to interpret them. To illustrate this, we will analyze graphics from the 2024 match between the USA and Pakistan in the ICC Men's T20 World Cup: one from the first innings and another from the second innings.

First Innings: Understanding the Score Graphic

1. Current Score:

- Pakistan's score is **152/7**, indicating they have scored 152 runs and lost 7 wickets. Some broadcasts may present the score as 7/152, while others will display it as 152/7.

- The additional detail "19.4 overs" indicates that 19 full overs and 4 deliveries have been bowled in the innings.

2. Batters at the Crease:

- Two batters are listed:
    - **Haris**: Scored 3 runs from 3 balls.
    - **Afridi**: Scored 16 runs from 14 balls and is the striker, meaning he is currently facing the bowler.

3. Bowler in Action:

- The bowler is **Ali-Khan**, and his stats are presented as follows:
    - Overs bowled: 3.4
    - Runs conceded: 23
    - Wickets taken: 1

4. Match Context:

- The text prominently displays "USA v PAK" and "ICC MEN'S T20 WORLD CUP," indicating the competing teams and the tournament.

- Pakistan is batting, as indicated by the active batters' statistics displayed next to the Pakistani flag.

5. Overs Tracker:

- A visual representation of the balls bowled in the current over is typically displayed as six circles. Empty circles indicate future deliveries, while the two filled circles represent two completed dot balls that have already been bowled in the 20th over. Any runs scored will be shown as a number within the circle, along with "W" for Wide and "NB" for No Ball. In the case of a Wide or No Ball, a seventh circle will appear.

Second Innings: Understanding the Score Graphic

The second innings graphic presents a similar structure but focuses on the chasing team's (USA) progress toward the target.

1. Current Score:

- USA's score is **104/1**, meaning they have scored 104 runs and lost 1 wicket.

- The additional detail "13 overs" indicates that 13 full overs have been bowled in the innings.

2. Target Information:

- The target score set by Pakistan in the first innings: **160 runs**. Pakistan scored 159 runs in the first innings therefore 160 is the target score for the USA to win.

3. Match Context

- The scoreboard shows that the USA needs 56 more runs to win and has 42 balls remaining. This information is crucial, as it outlines the chase scenario.

- To calculate the **required run rate**, divide the runs needed by the balls remaining and multiply by 6 (to account for overs). In this case, 56 runs divided by 42 balls remaining, multiplied by 6 balls per over, equals a required run rate of 8 runs per over.

Key Components of a Cricket Scoreboard

While the presentation may differ slightly between broadcasters, these key components are universal:

1. **Score Overview**: Displays the total runs and wickets for the batting team, often accompanied by overs bowled.

2. **Individual Performances**: Shows the statistics for the current batters and bowler.

3. **Match Context**: Highlights the competing teams, tournament name, and target score when relevant.

4. **Visual Aids**: Ball-by-ball trackers, team logos, and flags make the information more digestible and visually appealing.

The Takeaway

Scoreboards are designed to deliver comprehensive game updates, but they can appear complex to new viewers. By understanding the elements outlined here, you'll be able to interpret any cricket scoreboard with confidence, regardless of how it's presented on TV or online.

An Example Match: Bringing It All Together

Let's dive into an example game to see how it all plays out: my hometown team, the **Morrisville Raptors**, faces off against the **Seattle Thunderbolts**. The captains flip a coin, and the Thunderbolts win the toss. They choose to bat first, while the Raptors choose to bowl the first over from the Parking Lot side.

| Score: 0/0 0.0 | (0 wickets/outs, 0 runs, first over, zero balls delivered) |

Over #1, Ball 1

The first Raptor bowler delivers the ball, and the first Thunderbolt striker hits it into the deep outfield. It rolls to the boundary for **four** runs. The score is now 4-0, and the same batter is set to face the next ball.

Score: 0/4 0.1   (0 wickets/outs, 4 runs, first over, one ball delivered)

Over #1 Ball 2

The batter hits a ground ball that takes some time to field. Both batters sprint across the pitch to the opposite ends, scoring **one run**. The batting team now has **five runs**. With the batters having switched positions, the second batter (Batter #2) is now the active striker facing the bowler.

Score: 0/5 0.2   (0 wickets/outs, 5 runs, first over, two balls delivered)

Over #1 Ball 3

On the next ball, the batter realizes they cannot hit it cleanly. As the trajectory will carry the ball away from the stumps, they let it pass, and it is caught by the Keeper. Any legal ball that does not result in a run is called a **Dot Ball**. The score remains **5-0**, and the batters stay in their positions.

Score: 0/5 0.3   (0 wickets/outs, 5 runs, first over, three balls delivered)

Over #1 Ball 4

The fourth ball heads toward Batter #2's legs. If it hits their pads, the umpire might call them out for **Leg Before Wicket (LBW)** since the ball was in line with the stumps. To avoid this, the batter executes a defensive shot, hitting the ball straight into the ground, similar to a bunt in baseball. The ball is considered safe, and the batter lives to face the next ball.

Score: 0/5 0.4   (0 wickets/outs, 5 runs, first over, four balls delivered)

Over #1 Ball 5

Feeling confident, Batter #2 hits a pop fly into the outfield. The fielder near the boundary makes a spectacular diving catch, preventing the ball from touching the ground. The fielders celebrate wildly—this marks their first **wicket** (dismissal). The score is now **1-5** (1 wicket lost, 5 runs scored). Batter #2 walks off the field, crossing paths with Batter #3, who takes their place.

Score: 1/5 0.5 (1 wicket/out, 5 runs, first over, five balls delivered)

Over #1 Ball 6

Batter #3 steps in as the striker while Batter #1 remains the non-striker. The sixth ball is hit into the outfield and rolls toward the boundary. The non-striker sees an opportunity and urges the striker to run hard. They complete one run, then notice the fielder has mishandled the ball and decide to run again, securing **two runs**.

The fielder catches up and throws the ball toward the stumps, narrowly missing a run-out. The fielding team appeals, shouting **"howzat,"** but the umpire signals **Not Out**. The fielding team challenges the decision, sending the play to the **third umpire** in the replay booth for review. After examining the replay, the on-field umpire's decision stands. The score is now **1-7**, and the first of 20 overs is complete.

Score: 1/7 1.0 (1 wicket/out, 7 runs, 1st over is complete, 19 overs remaining)

The bowler collects their hat and sunglasses from the umpire and takes their position in the field. The Raptors' captain chooses a new bowler, who prepares to bowl from the opposite side of the pitch. Batter #1, once again the striker, gets ready to face the second bowler at the start of the second over.

The Second Innings

Let's skip ahead to the conclusion of the first innings. After 20 overs, the Thunderbolts are **4-155** (four wickets lost, 155 runs scored). This competitive total gives both sides a fair shot at victory. The Raptors now need **156 runs** to win or **155 runs** to force a **Super Over**.

Score: 4/155 20.0	(4 wickets/outs, 155 runs, end of first innings, Target 156)

The Thrilling Finish

Fast forward to the 18th over of the second innings. The Raptors have scored **153 runs** but lost **9 wickets**.

Score: 9/153 18.0	(9 wickets/outs, 153 runs, 18th over completed, Target 156)

The Thunderbolts can win the match by either getting one more batter out or preventing the Raptors from scoring their 156th run. The Raptors can clinch the game by reaching their target of 156 runs. How exciting it is that both teams have a chance to win on the next delivery!

The ninth Raptor batter faces the pressure head-on, sending the ball soaring over the boundary for a dramatic **Six**. The score leaps to **9-159**, and the Raptors are victorious. The last two overs are unnecessary, as the outcome has already been decided.

Another quirk of cricket is how final scores are reported. If the team batting in the second innings wins, their margin of victory is expressed as the number of wickets remaining— for example, "won by 2 wickets." Conversely, if they lose, the margin is described in terms of runs, such as "lost by 22 runs." In this example, the Morrisville Raptors won by 5 wickets. Familiarity with this terminology enhances understanding when interpreting match results.

Summary: Your Crash Course in Cricket

Believe it or not, you now have all the knowledge you need to watch a cricket match—whether on TV or in person—and follow the action. While many details and strategies will be explored later in this book, you don't need them to start enjoying games immediately.

As you watch a match, you will have many questions. While most answers can be found in the upcoming chapters, it's perfectly fine if some remain unanswered. Even lifelong football fans may struggle to fully grasp the nuances of an offensive line. Some concepts are best understood by players and the most devoted superfans.

At this stage, dive in and watch some cricket highlights or a full game. YouTube offers plenty of examples showcasing bowling, batting, and dismissals. To watch a complete game, search for "cricket match minor league cricket full game replay" and look for videos that are about 2-3 hours long. A U.S. minor league match is a great starting point.

As you watch, pay particular attention to **run rates**:

- In the first innings, note how many runs a team scores per over. For instance, if they score 20 runs after two overs, their run rate is 10. Maintaining this rate throughout the game would result in a final score of 200—an impressive total.

- In the second innings compare the batting team's current run rate to the required rate needed to achieve their target score. For example, if the target is 120 runs, they must score at a rate of 6 runs per over. If their current run rate is only 5, they will need to accelerate their scoring to stay on track. Conversely, if their run rate is 8, they are exceeding the required pace and will focus on maintaining their momentum. As the innings progresses, if the batting team falls behind the required run rate when they enter the **Death Overs** (overs 16-20), they are likely to adopt a highly aggressive batting approach to close the gap.

If the batting team struggles and scores only 89 runs in the first innings, expect an early finish. The second team can afford to be patient, requiring a **run rate** of just 4.5 runs per over. They'll likely aim for safe, consistent play, avoiding risks to ensure victory. On the other hand, if the first team scores a towering 192 runs, the batting team faces immense pressure in the second innings. Achieving such a high run rate demands aggressive batting, increasing the likelihood of wickets. The match is likely to end early if they lose 10 wickets before reaching 193 runs or completing 20 overs.

Most matches feature a nail-biting second innings, with both teams convinced they have a legitimate chance of clinching victory. This balance of uncertainty is what makes cricket so enthralling. You'll see teams valiantly defending low scores with precise bowling and tight fielding, while others unleash aggressive batting to chase down towering target scores. It's this dynamic interplay that keeps fans on the edge of their seats until the very last ball.

Translating the Game: Cricket Terms for Baseball Fans

Baseball Term	Cricket Term
Batting Average	Runs Per Over
Breaking Ball Pitcher	Spin Bowler, Spinner, Tweaker
Catcher	Wicketkeeper / Keeper
Earned Run Average	Bowling Average
Error	Misfield or "Put Down"
Fastball Pitcher	Fast Bowler / Swing Bowler
Force-Out	Run-Out

Ground Rule Double	Boundary / Four runs
Home Run	Sixer / Six runs
Infield	30 Yard Circle
Out	Wicket/Out
Picked Off	Stumped
Pitcher	Bowler
Plate	Stumps
Strike Zone	In line to hit the stumps/wicket
Throw	Delivery

Chapter Two

Discovering Cricket: Where and How to Watch

You are now ready to watch your first cricket match! So, what's next?

If you're fortunate enough to live near a venue that hosts major or minor league cricket, take the opportunity to check their schedules and weather forecasts to attend your first match in person. Alternatively, explore local cricket clubs that play whenever conditions allow—there are hundreds across the U.S. offering training sessions and inter-club competitions. Although these games may not take place in elaborate stadiums, they provide a uniquely inviting atmosphere, with friendly spectators often eager to share their knowledge and explain the intricacies of the game.

For a more convenient viewing experience, cricket can be enjoyed from the comfort of home. To explore past matches without committing to a subscription, YouTube offers an excellent selection of full game replays. Searching for **"cricket match full game Morrisville Raptors"** yields matches with American announcers, making the games both accessible and engaging. To save time, skip pregame discussions and breaks, allowing you to focus on the key moments of the match. This approach is ideal for learning about and appreciating cricket at your own pace.

For a more comprehensive and up-to-date experience, **Willow TV** stands out as the premier platform for exclusive cricket content. With matches occurring almost daily across the globe, cricket has evolved into a year-round sport. While time zone differences may prevent you from watching live, Willow TV offers full match replays divided by innings, providing the flexibility to catch the action whenever it suits you. Fortunately, cricket's niche following in the U.S. makes it unlikely that the results will be spoiled by a friend or text before you catch up!

What to Follow During a Match

When starting out, focus on the basics: the score, the number of overs bowled, the number of wickets fallen (outs), and the run rate. These core elements create an enjoyable match experience and provide a solid foundation for understanding the game. As the overs progress, try predicting the final score based on the current run rate. This adds an interactive element to your viewing experience and offers insight into how teams might strategize in the remaining overs.

When a wicket falls, pay close attention—dismissals often occur in clusters. It's not uncommon for the next batter to be dismissed on their very first ball, a situation known as a **golden duck**. If fielders vocally appeal for a wicket and the umpire disagrees, they remain motionless, delivering a clear and authoritative **non-decision**. As you watch more matches, you'll become familiar with the primary umpire signals, making it easier to recognize when they indicate an **out**, **boundary**, or **six**. For your convenience, a detailed overview of common umpire calls and signals will be provided later in the book, serving as a helpful reference whenever needed.

Initially, only caught fly balls are easy to spot. Don't be frustrated if you can't immediately understand why a player was dismissed. The announcers will explain it, and the replay will provide clarity. It takes time to grasp the reasons behind some dismissals in real-time, but you will feel proud of yourself as you start to recognize them.

As you continue your cricket-watching journey, explore one new aspect of the game at a time, starting with the art of bowling. Determine whether the bowler is a **fast bowler**, who delivers with pace and aims for lateral movement, or a **spin bowler**, who relies on guile and turn. Observe how much the ball moves side to side for fast bowlers, often influenced by swing or seam conditions. For spin bowlers, focus on how their delivery affects the ball's trajectory after bouncing, changing its direction and potentially deceiving the batter.

Pay attention to the bowler's tactics: are they targeting the batter's chest with short-pitched deliveries or the feet with precise yorkers? Try to discern the bowler's strategy: are they prioritizing wickets with aggressive deliveries or limiting runs by maintaining tight lines and lengths? To enhance your understanding of these nuances, refer to the corresponding chapter in this book, which offers detailed insights into bowling techniques and strategies.

Next, pay attention to the fielding. Why are so many fielders positioned closely together on the off side of the batter? How much training and skill does it take for a fielder to catch the ball while sliding or rolling on the ground? How sharp were the wicketkeeper's reflexes on that play? Would you have been able to reach the ball when the professional athlete could not? And how much would your hand sting if you had made that catch?

Then, dive deeper into the fascinating art of batting. Observe when batters choose offensive shots, aimed at scoring runs, versus defensive ones designed to protect their wicket. Notice how their technique adapts based on the type of bowler they face. Against fast bowlers, batters often rely on quick reflexes and solid footwork to manage pace and bounce, while facing spin bowlers typically demands greater patience and precision to counter deceptive turn and flight.

Pay attention to footwork—why do batters sometimes step forward onto their front foot versus leaning back onto their back foot? This usually depends on the ball's length: front-foot play is common for balls pitched up (fuller deliveries) that can be driven, while back-foot play is ideal for shorter deliveries, allowing for greater control and reaction time.

Finally, assess their level of aggression at various points in the match. Are they attacking to accelerate the run rate or playing cautiously to preserve wickets? Their approach often reflects the match situation, such as chasing a target, building a partnership, or countering pressure from an effective bowler. For further insights into batting techniques and strategies, refer to the corresponding chapter in this book to deepen your understanding.

You will notice the captain's strategic approach unfolding throughout the game. How are they structuring the order of bowlers and batters to enhance their team's chances of success? How deep is their bench in terms of skilled bowlers and batters, and how effectively are they utilizing this depth? Patience is an essential yet intangible quality for a captain—it's difficult to define, but as you observe their decisions under pressure, you will come to appreciate its significance even more.

Finally, take the next step by discovering your favorite teams and players. By this stage, their standout performances and unique styles should have already caught your attention. Tracking their progress adds an exciting personal connection to each match, whether it's monitoring a bowler's exceptional deliveries or admiring a batter's ability to chase a challenging total. Engaging with cricket at this level deepens your enjoyment of the game.

The dramatic and enthusiastic appeals from the fielding team, often accompanied by shouts and gestures, are another hallmark of cricket. When they believe they've dismissed a batter, these appeals can seem excessive at first glance. Players often perceive that louder and more theatrical appeals may sway the umpire, despite a lack of evidence supporting any correlation between volume and decision-making. Nevertheless, this tradition remains a lively and enduring aspect of the game.

Finding Cricket on TV and Streaming Services

Willow TV remains the gold standard for cricket coverage in the U.S. and Canada. Check if it's included in your cable or streaming package, as many providers offer free trials. If not, as of this writing subscriptions are available for $9.99 per month or $79.99 annually, providing an economical option for enthusiasts. Willow can be accessed on various platforms, including Roku®, tablets, and PCs.

For upcoming games, a convenient guide is displayed on the initial screen. The main Videos tab offers match replays, with T20 matches divided into two parts: part 1 for the first innings and part 2 for the second. While the interface may take some getting used to, the rich content makes the effort worthwhile.

English is the official language of cricket, so an English audio track with commentary is always available. Listening to commentary in a language you understand significantly enhances the viewing experience.

Willow's advertisements can test your patience. With a limited pool of sponsors, commercials tend to repeat frequently, though this may improve as more advertisers join the platform.

Willow Sports is a newly introduced ad-supported platform that provides sports content to viewers without requiring a subscription. Accessible through services like **Amazon Freevee**, **Sling Freestream**, **Fubo**, **Free Live Sports**, and **Plex**, this network is part of the Willow family, with a strong focus on cricket. The platform aims to introduce Americans and Canadians to cricket by offering free access to matches and events.

Currently, Willow Sports broadcasts **one event at a time**, featuring a curated selection of sports, including some that viewers may not have encountered before. As the platform evolves, there is hope that it will expand its offerings to include recorded content, further enhancing its utility for viewers. This service represents an exciting step in broadening cricket's reach across North America.

Watching a Match on TV

Watching a match live offers unmatched energy and atmosphere, while tuning in from home combines entertainment with unbeatable convenience. **Willow's full match replays** provide the flexibility to watch games at your preferred time or break them into manageable segments. For example, fans can skip directly to the 15th over to dive into the thrilling **Death Overs** (overs 15–20), known for aggressive batting, or focus solely on the second innings to savor the suspense of the run chase.

For many matches, it's not essential to watch every minute—especially since the second innings often determines the outcome. For less high-profile games, dedicating a full three hours may feel excessive. A great strategy for team-focused fans is to start with the coin toss to see whether their team will bat or bowl first. After that, they can watch only the innings featuring their team in the activity they enjoy most, whether it's batting or bowling. There's no obligation to watch the other innings, allowing for a more personalized and efficient viewing experience tailored to individual preferences and time constraints.

Allow yourself to turn off a game if you aren't enjoying it. If only 85 runs are scored in the first innings, you are unlikely to witness a nail-biter in the second innings. Conversely, if 250 runs are scored in the first innings, you probably won't miss out on the comeback of the century if you go for a walk instead.

Enjoy the announcers. They are typically former players and coaches who understand the game like no one else. Many are foreigners from an American perspective, which can be quite enjoyable. The differences between nationalities will become evident as they discuss the action. Don't be concerned if the announcers talk over your head; you don't need to know as much as they do, and you will learn more over time. They often reference cricket legends from the past, but don't worry if you don't recognize them; you're witnessing the cricket legends of the present. Even the co-announcers in the same booth frequently come from different nationalities, each rooting for their home teams, which adds to the entertainment.

The British announcers, in particular, are a joy to listen to, with their unique pronunciations and polite mannerisms. When deciding whether to review a call, listen for the expression "They are having a bit of a ponder." One player dove for a ball and came up limping, prompting the comment, "She has done herself a mischief."

Expect the weather to be an ever-present topic of conversation. Beyond cricket, social anthropologist Kate Fox found that 94% of Brits have discussed the weather within the last six hours, with 38% mentioning it in the past hour. Cricket is no exception; weather significantly influences the game, affecting conditions, strategies, and even outcomes. If you enjoy detailed weather discussions, cricket may be the perfect match for you!

You'll have the opportunity to learn Australia's colorful language, where you can put on your "sunnies" to enjoy a "brekkie" at "Maccas" while you fend off bites from a "mozzie." Watching a match held in Australia is a unique delight, especially when the field is filled with "Bin Chickens" loitering around before fluttering out of the way of an incoming ball or a determined fielder.

Wickets are pivotal moments in a cricket match and are frequently replayed multiple times during broadcasts to analyze the skill of the bowler or the error of the batter. However, these replays are not always preceded by a clear warning, which can confuse viewers who might mistake the replay for live action. While wickets are even more significant in longer formats such as ODIs and Test matches—where they can dramatically shift momentum—they remain crucial in T20 cricket as well, shaping the game's course by slowing run rates or exposing less experienced batters down the order.

During certain broadcasts, it may initially seem as though the announcers are noisily munching on Captain Crunch cereal with their microphones left on, creating an unprofessional impression. However, this sound often originates from an open microphone near the wicket, which captures the batters rubbing their feet on the ground to clean their cleats. Once this realization sets in, the noise becomes much less noticeable and easier to ignore.

Broadcasters often equip team captains or players with engaging personalities with microphones, allowing for brief yet insightful exchanges during the match. These moments give viewers unique perspectives on the game, offering a closer look at the players' strategies, thoughts, and emotions as the action unfolds.

The lively atmosphere is further enhanced by music and enthusiastic fan cheering throughout the game. Expect to hear **Sweet Caroline** as frequently as at a baseball game—it's a unifying moment, with fans from around the globe joining in to sing along to this iconic American tune.

Watching cricket offers flexibility, making multitasking perfectly acceptable. Key moments are regularly replayed during the broadcast, ensuring you never miss any action. Additionally, the option to rewind and relive exciting plays adds to the convenience and enjoyment of watching from home.

Watching a Live Match

Checking the weather ahead of time is essential, as it can prevent unnecessary travel; weather is often considered the enemy of cricket. The sun largely dictates what items to bring to an in-person match.

Selecting the right seat is crucial for an enjoyable experience. Ensure the seat offers a clear view of the main scoreboard or video screen for tracking stats, replays, and DRS reviews. A side-on view, perpendicular to the pitch, provides excellent visibility of fielders' positions and the batter's shot placements, while also allowing observation of the running between the wickets. An elevated perspective gives a broader view of the entire field. Some sections may attract more families with children, so choosing a seating area that matches individual preferences can enhance the experience.

Comfort is essential during a three-hour match, especially at larger venues with stadium seating. For added convenience, consider investing in a portable seat specifically designed for stadium benches. These seats provide extra cushioning and support for longer durations. To stay cool and protect yourself from the sun, small umbrellas that clamp onto metal seats are a practical choice.

At smaller venues, bringing a comfortable camping chair is highly recommended to enhance your experience. Chairs equipped with canopies offer effective sun protection and reduce glare. Staying aware of the sun is crucial during day games—seek out shaded areas or spots that will gain shade as the match progresses. On particularly sunny days, portable fans and insulated water bottles can help keep you refreshed and hydrated throughout the event.

While some games may feature food trucks, bringing personal food and drinks is a safe option. Verify whether alcohol is permitted at the venue, as policies vary. Major league matches often enforce clear bag policies for security inspections at the entrance.

Proper sun protection is crucial. Wearing a UV-blocking hat and applying ample sunscreen can prevent "cricket burns" and other sun-related damage. While binoculars might not be used frequently, they can enhance the viewing experience when needed. Sunglasses, or "sunnies," as Australians say, are indispensable for shielding the eyes and improving comfort during outdoor matches.

Sight screens, located behind each bowler, play a vital role in providing a clear background for batters to track the ball. These screens adjust based on the ball color: black for white balls and white for red balls. **Walking in front of the sight screens is strictly discouraged,** as it halts play and draws disapproval from both players and fans.

Finally, the best companions for a cricket match are partners, friends, and kids. While enjoying a match solo can be beneficial for learning the sport, sharing the experience with others adds to the fun, particularly on a sunny day spent outdoors.

Chapter Three

The Art of Batting

Bowlers are impressive, but batting is where the glory lies!

For a comprehensive and expert tutorial on batting, it's best to consult specialized resources. However, a deep understanding of batting isn't necessary to enjoy watching skilled batters in action.

Memorizing every type of shot and identifying them during a match is not required. While this knowledge can enhance your appreciation of the game, it may feel overwhelming. What's important is recognizing that the batter stands in the center of the field and can hit the ball in any direction. There are no points awarded for style—only runs count.

Every player brings a unique approach to their batting technique. Major golf tournaments feature the best golfers in the world teeing off from the same spot, yet their swings vary significantly. Similarly, cricket batters display distinctive styles and innovative methods, each contributing to the rich diversity and artistry of the sport.

When observing the batter, note whether they are playing a defensive shot to stay in the game or an offensive shot aimed at scoring runs. Pay attention to where they direct the ball. They may aim to hit it through the infield along the ground, target a gap in the outfield, or hit it over the boundary for a six. Sometimes, their goal is simply to secure a safe single, while at other times, their focus shifts entirely to scoring boundaries and sixes.

Batting comes with intense pressure, as all eyes in the stadium focus on the batter. The batter faces a direct confrontation against the bowler and the combined efforts of the ten fielders supporting them. Success often depends on strategic preparation: the batter studies a scouting report that outlines the bowler's playing style, tendencies, and weaknesses. At the same time, the batter must adapt to immediate factors, such as the pitch condition, the wear on the ball, and the anticipated speed of the ball as it travels through the outfield.

The bowler's run-up provides clues, such as how the ball is gripped. Observing their motion and release technique helps predict the ball's speed, spin, and trajectory. The batter must subconsciously perform differential calculus to determine the ball's expected arrival time, bounce point, rebound height, and horizontal position—all within a fraction of a second.

After these rapid evaluations, the batter has approximately 0.36 seconds to decide how to respond. If the decision is to play a shot and score runs, the next step involves selecting the appropriate shot: drive, cut, pull, hook, or sweep. This choice influences adjustments to stance and grip. Depending on the ball's delivery, the batter may stand firm on the back foot for stability or step forward to meet the ball for a stronger hit. With no restrictions on direction, creative shots like scooping the ball over the head to land behind are possible.

Once the ball is struck, there is no time to pause and admire the hit. The batter must listen for instructions from the non-striker on whether to run or stay in place. While running, a quick glance at the ball's trajectory helps determine whether to attempt additional runs. If a fielder aims a throw toward the wicket, it's crucial to reach the popping crease before the bails are dislodged. The decision to ground the bat while running or slide headfirst must account for safety and efficiency. Should a disagreement with the umpire arise, the batter may need to clearly recall the events to decide whether to use the team's single review to continue batting.

Strategic decisions are heavily influenced by the match situation. When the run rate falls behind in the late overs, an aggressive approach becomes crucial to bridge the gap. Conversely, if the target is modest and the team is comfortably ahead, a conservative strategy to preserve wickets is often preferred. The number of fallen wickets also significantly shapes the game plan; for example, when the tenth batter, who is typically less skilled, comes to the crease, they face higher stakes and must carefully balance the need to protect their wicket with contributing to the team's total.

The condition and ability of the non-striker are equally pivotal in determining tactics. When paired with the eleventh batter at the end of the lineup, strategies usually focus on maximizing opportunities for the stronger batter. This might involve deliberately avoiding singles to keep the more capable player facing the bowler. Additionally, factors such as the non-striker's pace or any injuries must be considered when making running decisions, ensuring the team minimizes unnecessary risks while capitalizing on scoring opportunities.

During a match, Indian star cricketer KL Rahul was struggling, missing every ball and becoming increasingly frustrated. As the bowler walked back, Rahul turned to the wicketkeeper and said, "Phew... What couldn't I do with a bottle of beer?" The wicketkeeper cheekily replied, "Hit it with the bat?"

The Cricket Bat: Your Weapon of Choice

Bats are traditionally crafted from specific varieties of White Willow, commonly known as Cricket Bat Willow (Salix alba var. caerulea). This wood is highly valued for its unique combination of toughness, shock resistance, and lower tendency to dent or splinter. Its lightweight nature further enhances its suitability for bat-making. Among the different types, Kashmir Willow is a more economical choice, while English Willow, recognized for its superior quality, is the preferred option for professional-level bats.

Cricket bats are available in various sizes and weights to suit batters of different ages and body types. Regular maintenance—such as cleaning, oiling, and a process known as **knocking-in**, which is similar to breaking in a baseball glove—is essential for preserving a bat. With proper care, a quality bat can last a lifetime. Introductory bats range from $60 to $150, while professional-quality bats are priced between $200 and $600+.

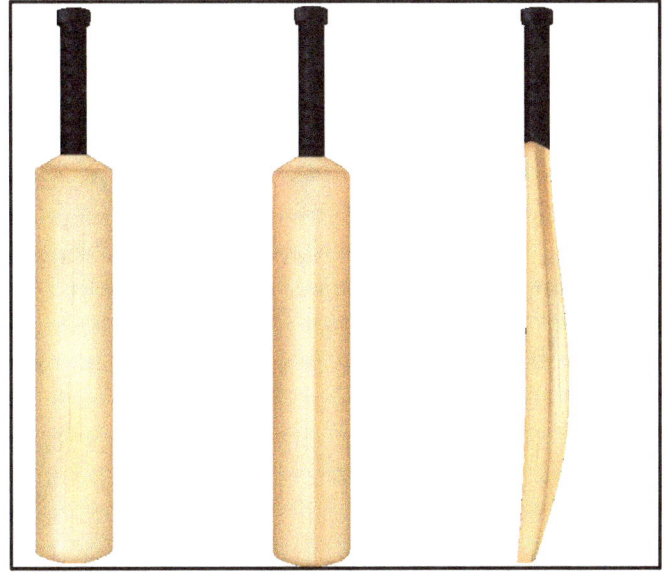

The blade, the flat-fronted section crafted specifically for striking the ball, is connected to a long cylindrical cane handle through a splice. This vital joint plays a key role in ensuring both the bat's durability and the efficient transfer of energy during play. For enhanced comfort and control, the handle is typically wrapped with a rubber grip.

On the striking side, the blade is flat, while the back features a ridge that boosts strength and power. The slightly rounded edges serve to minimize the risk of breakage during intense use. Additionally, the handle is designed to absorb the impact shock from each hit, providing the batter with a smoother and more comfortable playing experience.

A right-handed batter holds the cricket bat with their left hand at the bottom of the handle and their right hand above it. The left hand provides most of the control, while the right hand contributes guidance and power. The hands are kept close together, with the knuckles of both hands aligned.

Precision in striking the ball is less critical in cricket than in sports like golf. A batter may miss the sweet spot of the bat, causing the ball to hit the edge and rebound in unexpected directions. Surprisingly, this can be advantageous, as these unpredictable deflections often catch fielders off guard, increasing the chances of scoring runs. Interestingly, many batters may be reluctant to acknowledge how often runs result from these unintentional contacts, adding a touch of subtle humor to the sport's dynamics.

Similar to baseball, the faster the ball approaches, the quicker it rebounds off the bat. To limit runs, fast bowlers may deliberately slow their deliveries, making it harder for batters to achieve boundaries and sixes. When defending a significant lead, bowlers can afford to concede singles, prioritizing control over big scoring plays.

Mastering Cricket Shots

Understanding the terminology for the left and right sides of a batter is essential. These designations vary depending on whether the batter is right-handed or left-handed. For a **right-handed batter**, the area to their **right** is called the **Off Side**, while the area to their **left** is referred to as the **Leg Side**. Conversely, for a **left-handed batter**, these terms are reversed: the **Off Side** is on their **left**, and the **Leg Side** is on their **right**. This distinction is crucial for accurately d escribing field placements, strategies, and shot directions.

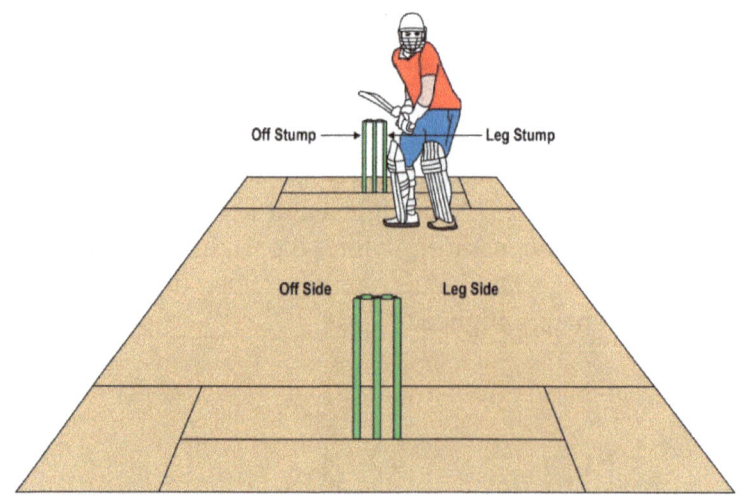

Batters in baseball must remain within the batter's box, where stability and precision are crucial. In contrast, cricket batters have greater freedom of movement. They are not confined to a static position and can move within the crease or even step out of it while the bowler delivers the ball. This mobility enables cricket batters to execute a wide variety of shots.

Unlike other bat-and-ball games, cricket batters can hit the ball in any direction, which fosters creativity in their striking. They can swing for the fences or aim for singles, typically targeting open areas of the field where there are no nearby fielders.

Batting begins with the stance: feet should be shoulder-width apart for a solid foundation, with knees slightly bent to position the batter in an attack stance. Most of the weight starts on the back foot but shifts forward as the ball approaches. The hands are raised near the back shoulder, maintaining a firm yet relaxed grip on the bat. The head remains steady, eyes level, and all attention is focused on the bowler's release point. The batter lifts the bat vertically in preparation for hitting, known as the **backlift**. Batters will move forward or backward depending on the ball's trajectory.

A forward movement constitutes a **front foot shot**, with weight placed on the front foot. This shot is typically used for balls bowled long, arriving between ankle and thigh height. The batter steps forward, bends their front knee, and brings the bat down to the anticipated height of the ball. Hitting the ball closer to the bounce point reduces the effects of spin.

A **back foot shot** is utilized when the ball is bowled short, bouncing above the thigh but below the head. The batter steps back and may even stand on tiptoes to raise the bat to the ball's height. By stepping back, the batter gains a small amount of extra time for adjustments while remaining in the popping crease, thus avoiding being run out by a wicketkeeper's catch.

For **vertical shots**, the bat is swung in a straight arc, typically to play deliveries pitched closer to the batter. In contrast, **horizontal shots**, or **cross-bat shots**, involve swinging the bat horizontally and are often used for shorter-pitched balls.

The most common cricket shots are categorized into vertical and horizontal strokes:

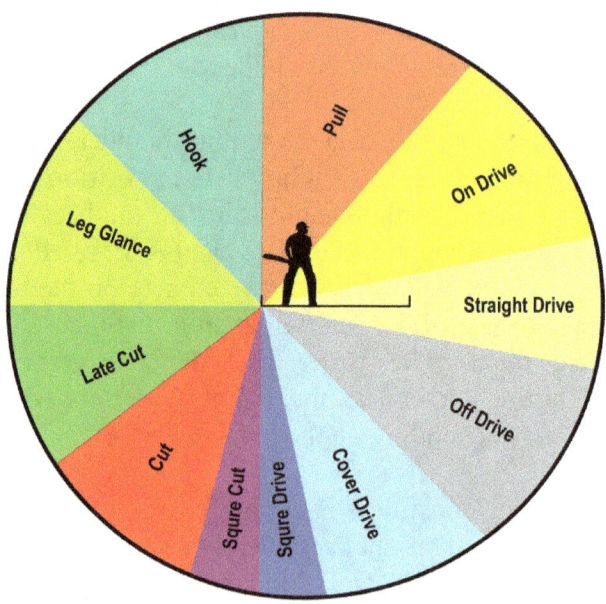

Vertical Shot: Straight Drive

The batter steps forward with the front leg and angles the top of the bat toward the ground during the swing, keeping the hands relatively vertical on the handle. The ball is struck in front of the batter and driven straight along the ground to minimize the risk of being caught.

Vertical Shot: Defensive Shot/Block Stroke

This defensive technique focuses on preventing the ball from hitting the pads or the stumps. The batter holds the bat loosely to absorb the ball's impact, applying no power to the stroke.

- **Forward Defensive**: Played by stepping forward to meet the ball close to the ground.

- **Backward Defensive**: Played by drawing the front foot back and contacting the ball at a higher position while standing fairly upright.

Vertical Shot: Leave

While not technically a shot, this involves the batter deliberately holding the bat out of the way to let the ball pass when they judge it won't hit the stumps or pads. If the ball isn't caught by the wicketkeeper and runs past, the batters might attempt to take a run.

Vertical Shot: Push

Similar to a defensive stroke but with the intention of deflecting the ball into an unprotected area of the field.

Vertical Shot: Flick

A stroke used for balls pitched on the leg side. The batter uses their wrists to flick the ball toward the field, also known as a **clip off the legs**. This shot can be played off either foot, with the bat angled toward the leg side.

Horizontal Shot: Cut

Typically used against a short-pitched ball that is wide of the stumps, the batter makes contact as the ball passes by, using the bowler's pace to divert it.

Horizontal Shot: Square Drive

This stroke is similar to the cut shot, with the batter bending their knees and crouching low to make contact near the ground. Played off the front foot, the batter steps toward the ball and uses their wrists to guide it to the desired part of the field.

Horizontal Shot: Pull and Hook Shots

The pull shot resembles a typical baseball swing, executed across the body when the ball is around waist height, in a horizontal arc. It becomes a hook shot when the ball bounces at or above chest height. Both pull and hook shots can be played off either the front or back foot.

Horizontal Shot: Sweep

The popular sweep shot requires the batter to drop to their front knee while swinging in a horizontal arc to **Sweep** the ball into the field. This shot is particularly effective against spin bowlers, allowing the batter to direct the ball into advantageous locations away from fielders, making it valuable for scoring runs.

Indian cricketer MS Dhoni is renowned for his unorthodox "helicopter shot," which features a distinctive wrist flick that sends the ball soaring over midwicket. The follow-through of this shot resembles the blades of a helicopter. As one commentator remarked, "If cricket doesn't work out for him, he could always become a helicopter pilot!"

Edging refers to situations where the ball makes contact with the edge of the bat instead of the middle, often resulting in unpredictable outcomes. Here are the common types of edges and their effects:

- **Outside Edge**: The ball strikes the outer edge of the bat, farthest from the batter's body. These edges often fly toward the wicketkeeper or slip fielders, creating catching opportunities.

- **Inside Edge**: The ball strikes the inner edge of the bat, closest to the batter's body. This commonly results in deflections onto the stumps, leading to a bowled dismissal, or sends the ball toward leg-side fielders.

- **Bottom Edge**: The ball makes contact with the bottom edge of the bat. These edges typically drop straight to the ground but may also deflect onto the stumps, resulting in a bowled dismissal.

- **Top Edge**: The ball hits the top edge of the bat, usually causing it to fly high into the air. This gives fielders an excellent opportunity to catch the ball and claim a wicket.

- **Leading Edge**: The ball makes contact with the leading edge of the bat—the edge facing the direction of the shot. These edges often pop up in the air, creating easy catching opportunities for the fielders.

Running Between the Wickets

Running between the wickets is a fundamental aspect of cricket that occurs frequently but is often underappreciated in discussions. It is a critical contributor to scoring and often leads to thrilling run-out scenarios.

A batter is **In Their Ground** if any part of their body or bat, held in hand, is touching the ground behind the popping crease. This position ensures safety from being run out or stumped. Conversely, a batter is **Out of Their Ground** if neither their body nor their bat is behind the popping crease, leaving them vulnerable to dismissal.

Running with pads may appear cumbersome, and understandably so, as the pads add weight and restrict movement. However, studies reveal that running three runs while wearing pads increases the time required by only 0.5 seconds compared to running without them.

Turning refers to the quick movement runners make when reversing direction at the end of a run to start the next one. Efficient turning—whether through a pivot or an arcing motion—minimizes time lost and helps maintain momentum. The precision of the turn can often determine whether a batter secures an additional run or risks being run out.

To avoid dismissal, batters must **ground their bat** across the crease. This involves sliding the bat into the ground as they approach the popping crease to ensure it is safely behind the line. If the bat is grounded and subsequently lifted off the ground, the batter cannot be dismissed.

Commentators frequently analyze **partnerships**, evaluating how well batters complement each other in terms of communication and running styles. Selecting pairs in the lineup often involves pairing players whose strengths align. For instance, a fast runner paired with a slower runner can only achieve runs within the capabilities of the slower runner.

Miscommunication is a common challenge when running between the wickets, as one runner may attempt a run while the other remains in their crease. Overconfidence can worsen these errors, leading to high-risk decisions and an underestimation of the speed and precision of the fielders.

Clear and effective communication is essential for minimizing such mishaps. Typically, the non-striker initiates the running call after the ball is struck, but both players must actively communicate their intentions. Standard calls such as **"yes," "no,"** and **"wait"** are universally used to streamline decision-making. Proper coordination not only prevents mid-pitch collisions but also significantly reduces the chances of unnecessary run-outs, ensuring smoother gameplay and better utilization of scoring opportunities.

While running, batters constantly scan the field, searching for gaps and analyzing the abilities of opposing fielders. Judging the ball's speed and trajectory is equally crucial for making running decisions.

Stealing Singles is an aggressive running tactic designed to score runs off nearly every delivery. By turning singles into doubles, this strategy keeps pressure on the fielding side. However, such aggression often results in extremely close plays, with the runner needing to beat the ball to the wicket by mere fractions of a second.

With two runners, the bowler, and possibly the wicketkeeper all occupying the pitch, things can become crowded. Batters have the right of way, and fielders must avoid obstructing their path. Intentional obstruction by a fielder may result in penalty runs awarded to the batting side. Conversely, batters must not deliberately obstruct a fielder. If either batter obstructs a fielder attempting a catch, the batter currently on strike will be given out—even if the obstruction is caused by the non-striker.

Runners must also avoid stepping into the **Protected Area** or **Danger Area**, a virtual rectangle starting five feet in front of the stumps at each end and four feet wide. This rule is in place to maintain the pitch's condition. Bowlers are also prohibited from entering this area.

Understanding Batting Statistics

The primary statistic for a batter is the Batting Average, calculated by dividing the number of runs scored by the number of times dismissed. To be successful, a batter must score many runs while minimizing dismissals—easier said than done.

The Australian legend Sir Don Bradman is widely regarded as the greatest batter of all time. He scored a total of 6,996 runs over 52 Test matches and was dismissed only 70 times, resulting in a Batting Average of 6,996/70 = 99.94. To put his achievement in perspective, his average was 38 points higher than that of the next greatest batter.

The following are key statistics that measure batters:

- **Runs Scored**: The total number of runs a batter has accumulated.

- **Batting Average**: Calculated by dividing the total number of runs scored by the number of times the batter has been dismissed, representing a batter's consistency.

- **Strike Rate**: Measures the scoring rate, calculated as runs scored per 100 balls faced.

- **Centuries:** The number of times a batter has scored 100 or more runs in a single innings.

- **Half-Centuries**: The number of times a batter has scored between 50 and 99 runs in a single innings.

- **Balls Faced**: The total number of balls a batter has faced.

- **Highest Score**: The highest individual score a batter has achieved in a single innings.

- **Fours and Sixes**: The number of boundaries (fours) and over-boundaries (sixes) hit by the batter.

- **Innings Played**: The total number of innings in which the batter has participated.

- **Not Outs**: The number of times the batter remained not out at the end of an innings.

- **Boundaries per Innings**: The average number of boundaries hit per innings played.

- **Dot Ball Percentage**: The percentage of dot balls (balls faced without scoring any runs) faced by the batter.

- **Partnership Runs**: The total number of runs scored in partnerships involving the batter.

- **Partnership Average**: The average number of runs scored in partnerships involving the batter.

Batting: Beyond the Basics

Additional batting information and edge cases:

Above all, a batter does not want to be **Out for a Duck**, meaning they have not scored any runs and have been dismissed. Instead, they aim to be **Off the Mark** by scoring their first run.

When a player hits the ball to a fielder who catches it, the batter is **Caught Out**. If the catch is made by the wicketkeeper, the batter is considered **Caught Behind**.

You will notice large walls on either side of the field in line with each bowler. These are the **Sight Screens** to provide a clear background for the batter to see the ball. These screens are adjusted based on the color of the ball (black for white balls and white for red balls). Play is stopped when an errant fan walks in front of the wall, a common occurrence in the U.S.; this is a lesson that new fans need to learn.

In a T20 match, the first six overs are known as the **Power Play**, a period designed to encourage aggressive batting. During this time, fielding restrictions permit only two players outside the 30-yard circle. With fewer fielders positioned deep, batters have an easier time hitting boundaries and seizing scoring opportunities, making the Power Play a crucial phase for establishing a strong start. Teams often leverage this advantage to set the tone for their innings and accumulate quick runs.

When a wicket falls, the incoming batter must be ready to take the crease within 90 seconds. If the incoming batter fails to arrive at the crease in time, they can be timed out, resulting in their dismissal.

During the 1983 Cricket World Cup, in India's match against Zimbabwe, cricketer Syed Kirmani was making toast in the dressing room when he was called to pad up. At first, he thought it was a joke. However, when he realized the team was in trouble, sitting at 5-17, he dropped his toast and got ready. Unfortunately, the toaster caused a fire, delaying the game by 30 minutes while firefighters were called to extinguish the flames.

If the ball hits the batter's body or protective equipment (excluding the arm, as it is considered part of the bat when playing a shot) without touching the bat, and the umpire determines that the ball would have hit the stumps had the batter not been in the way, they are dismissed **Leg Before Wicket (LBW)**. The dismissal (LBW) is based on the umpire's decision regarding whether the ball would have hit the stumps had it not been obstructed by the batter.

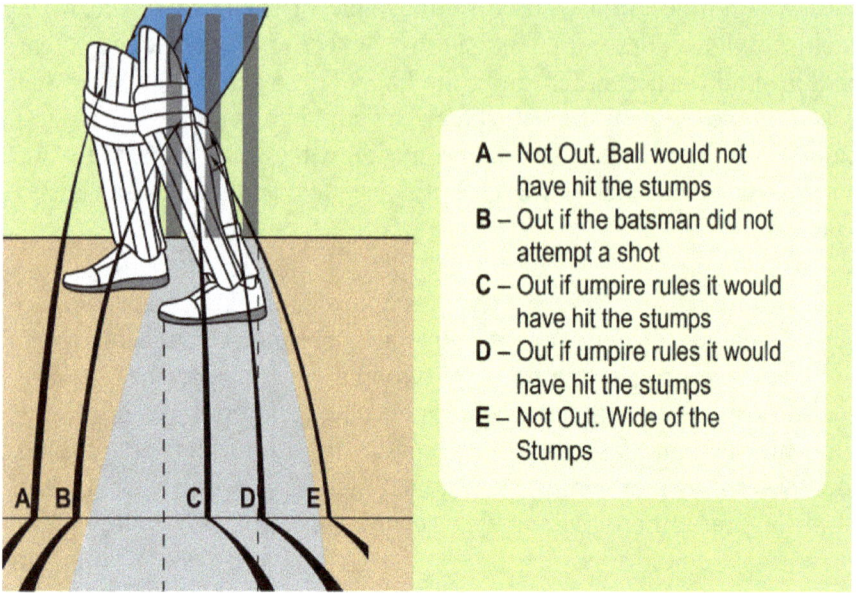

A – Not Out. Ball would not have hit the stumps
B – Out if the batsman did not attempt a shot
C – Out if umpire rules it would have hit the stumps
D – Out if umpire rules it would have hit the stumps
E – Not Out. Wide of the Stumps

Leg Byes (LB) are awarded as **Extras** when the ball deflects off the batter's body or protective equipment, provided the batter is either attempting a shot or trying to avoid being hit. This allows the runners to take runs between the wickets, contributing to the team's total without crediting the batter or bowler. However, if the ball strikes the batter's arm while attempting a shot, and the arm is holding the bat, it is considered part of the bat and not a Leg Bye. If the batter neither attempts a shot nor avoids the ball, no Leg Byes are awarded, and the ball is deemed dead.

If the bowler oversteps the crease, the umpire will call it a **no-ball (NB).** A no-ball can also be called if the bowler delivers the ball to the batter without it bouncing on the pitch, which is known as a **Full Toss** or **In The Full**. If the ball reaches the batter below the waist while they are in their normal stance, it is considered a legal delivery. However, if the ball reaches the batter at or above the waist, it is deemed a no-ball due to the potential danger it poses. These deliveries are often easier to hit but are used sparingly to surprise the batter.

If the bowler **oversteps the crease**, the umpire will call it a **no-ball (NB)**, as this violates bowling regulations. A no-ball can also be called for a **Full Toss**, which is a delivery that reaches the batter without bouncing on the pitch. If a Full Toss reaches the batter **below the waist** in their normal stance, it is considered a **legal delivery**. However, if it reaches the batter **at or above the waist**, it is deemed a **no-ball** due to the risk of injury from such deliveries. While Full Toss deliveries can be easier to hit, they are typically used sparingly to catch the batter off guard.

If the ball passes the batter without touching the bat, pads, or body, and the wicketkeeper does not stop it, the batters can run between the wickets for additional runs. If the ball reaches the boundary, it counts as four runs. These runs contribute to the team total, but the batter does not receive personal credit.

If the ball passes the batter too wide or too high for them to reach, the umpire will extend both arms sideways, ruling it a Wide Ball (WB). The batting team is awarded a run, which is not credited to the batter, and the bowler must deliver an additional ball.

An effective strategy for setting up the batting order is to have both a left-handed and a right-handed batter together. This may disrupt the bowler's rhythm, as they must adjust their line and length when facing batters of different stances. The fielding team must also make significant placement adjustments for each batter, potentially creating additional gaps in the field.

Unlike in baseball, the captain of the batting team can change the order of batters during the game. If they anticipate that spin bowlers will be active, they may send in a batter who handles spin effectively. The fielding team can also change their bowlers after each over to match the batters. However, as the game progresses, the fielding team captain loses some flexibility, as each bowler is allowed to bowl only four overs.

Batters face the bowler in a one-on-one contest, but opportunities for advice and encouragement abound. After an over or a boundary/six, the two active batters often come together to share insights about pitch conditions, bowlers' strategies, fielders' positions, and other tactical observations. These moments include congratulations and motivational support, not only from the partner batter but also from the rest of the team in the dugout.

All eleven players may be required to bat, with the lower-order batters typically being the weakest in the lineup. Bowlers tend to adopt more aggressive tactics to dismiss the final wickets and conclude the innings quickly. When the 10th and 11th batters exceed expectations, it can be immensely satisfying for them, as they defy the odds and make meaningful contributions to their team's performance.

When a batter is injured while batting, they can temporarily leave the game for treatment, a situation known as **Retired Hurt/Ill**. The next batter in the lineup replaces them and continues the innings from where the injured player left off. If the injured batter recovers, they are allowed to resume their batting position after a wicket falls, provided the innings is still ongoing.

If a player leaves the game for reasons other than injury, referred to as **Retired Out**, they may only return to bat with the permission of the opposing captain. Regardless of the circumstances, the batter remains eligible to participate as a fielder in the next innings.

Concussions are taken very seriously. Batters are particularly vulnerable to head injuries from being hit by the ball, which is why they wear specially designed helmets. A concussion protocol is in place to ensure that players at risk leave the field for medical attention. The umpire will also inspect the helmet for damage and instruct the batter to obtain a new one if necessary.

There is a batting phenomenon known as the **Nervous Nineties**. When a batter reaches 90 runs, they often start thinking about achieving a century (100 runs), making them more prone to getting out due to this distraction.

Batting strategy shifts significantly during the **Death Overs**, which refer to the last 4-5 overs of an innings. In the first innings Death Overs, batters aim to set the highest possible score to add pressure to the opposing team in their innings. In the second innings Death Overs, batters are aware of the runs needed and the balls remaining. If they are behind, they tend to become very aggressive, as the game is at stake. If only a few wickets have fallen, batters may take greater risks, knowing that another capable batter is ready to step in if they get out.

The most dangerous ball a batter will face is their first delivery; it is astonishing how often batters are bowled out on the first ball they face. This is because the bowler tends to be more aggressive, while the batter lacks the rhythm that comes with facing multiple deliveries.

A batter is dismissed as **Hit Wicket** if they dislodge the bails by striking the wicket with their bat, foot, body, or pads while the ball is in play.

A **Bye** occurs when the normally reliable wicketkeeper fails to catch the ball after it passes the batter, allowing it to run toward the boundary. The batters can then run between the wickets. Any runs scored, including boundaries, count toward the total score but do not affect the bowler's figures or the batter's statistics.

The batter can protect the wicket by hitting the ball with the bat. If it then rolls towards the wicket, they can use any part of their body except the hand not holding the bat to keep the ball from hitting the wicket for a dismissal. If they use their non-batting hand, the umpire will determine whether it was intentional or accidental. If intentional, they are given an out for **Obstructing the Field**.

When an innings concludes, the batter that was not dismissed is said to have been **All Out**. This is helpful for their batting average.

Chapter Four

The Science of Bowling

"Batting wins you games, but bowling wins you tournaments." — **Dale Steyn**

Watching a cricket match inevitably highlights the compelling duel between the bowler and the batter. While fans may focus on their preferred team's players, understanding the bowler's role enriches the experience and enhances appreciation for the sport. Over time, enthusiasts naturally gravitate toward their favorite bowlers, recognizing their unique styles and skills. Although detailed knowledge of bowling is valuable, new viewers are encouraged to initially focus on the broader game flow—runs scored and wickets taken. An appreciation for finer details, such as the intrigue of a Googly, comes with familiarity.

At its essence, bowling is the act of delivering the ball to the batter in a legal manner, aiming to restrict runs and take wickets. By dismissing batters, bowlers disrupt the opposing team's lineup, remove key players, and increase pressure on those who follow. This crucial role directly influences the team's ability to secure victory.

Cricket features a diverse array of bowlers, each with distinct skill sets and deliveries that often come with creative and amusing names. The dynamics of the pitch and ground surface can vary significantly, even from one day to the next on the same field. The captain plays a vital role in selecting bowlers strategically, relying on experience to adapt to the match's demands. Each bowler brings a unique style, from their run-up to their grip on the ball and the delivery techniques in their arsenal. Speed, accuracy, and adaptability further define their effectiveness. For example, England's Sophie Ecclestone stands out as the leading women's bowler globally, exemplifying the remarkable individuality that characterizes great bowlers.

Bowling strategy shares similarities with baseball's pitching decisions. When the National League introduced the Designated Hitter rule, many purists lamented the loss of managerial tactics surrounding pitchers having to bat. They relished the excitement of pitchers contributing offensively and the irreversible decisions managers faced when replacing them. The nuanced thrill of pitchers excelling as batters added layers to the game. Similarly, cricket captains navigate this strategic complexity, particularly in their bowling rotations. Some bowlers excel with the bat, while others are placed lower in the batting order—often at the 10th or 11th position—due to their primary focus on bowling rather than batting prowess.

Managing Time in Bowling

T20 matches are designed to last approximately three hours, requiring the bowling team to maintain a pace of at least 14.11 overs per hour. Failure to meet this target results in penalties, such as requiring an additional fielder to remain inside the circle for the remainder of the innings. Some leagues also penalize teams by awarding extra runs to the batting side.

The captain plays a pivotal role in ensuring that bowlers maintain the required pace. Interestingly, relying on five "fast" bowlers can hinder time management despite their quicker deliveries, as their extended run-ups and walk-backs consume valuable time. This underscores the importance of mixing fast and spin bowlers to manage time effectively.

Leagues provide opportunities for strategic time management through breaks:

- **Strategic Timeouts**: Teams are permitted one or two timeouts per innings, lasting 2-3 minutes each, for planning and tactical adjustments.

- **Innings Break**: A break of 10-15 minutes occurs between innings, during which teams switch roles.

- **Drink Breaks**: Brief 2-3 minute breaks allow players to rehydrate and refresh. In particularly hot conditions, umpires may grant additional drink breaks.

Effective time management is not just a rule but a critical aspect of strategy, enabling teams to maintain focus and momentum throughout the match.

Using the New Ball Effectively

In baseball, more than 100 balls are typically used in a single game. Fans may cherish the chance to own one of these prized $7 balls, but pitchers often prefer balls with slight natural scuffs, as they offer better grip and control. If an umpire notices a ball that is excessively damaged, it is promptly removed from play and replaced with a fresh one from their supply. Dedicated fans, remaining true to tradition, often throw back home run balls hit by the opposing team as a demonstration of loyalty to their side.

In cricket, the ideal scenario is to use the same ball for all 20 overs in a T20 innings. Cricket balls have their own lifecycle; new balls behave differently than those that are broken in. Spinners prefer a roughed-up ball, as it enhances their bowling strategy. They polish one side of the ball with their shirt while leaving the other side shiny, allowing for different rotations that make it challenging for batters to predict the delivery. A broken-in ball not only looks different but also undergoes a change in hardness, starting out hard and softening with use. Spin bowlers typically favor a softer ball, so fast bowlers usually bowl the first few overs to condition the ball for the spinners. The hardness of the ball works to their advantage, as they focus more on speed and control than on creating deceptive movements. A hard ball will bounce higher and travel faster, making it easier to control its lateral swing.

Fielders easily retrieve balls from individual runs and boundaries. However, sixes present a unique challenge, as the ball often lands beyond the boundary. In most cases, it ends up in an accessible area where the nearest person can retrieve it and throw it back into play. When the ball lands in the stands, fans, eager to be on camera, enthusiastically toss it back to a fielder. Although their throws may lack the precision and power of a professional's, they are delivered with far more joy. This tradition of returning the ball, rather than attempting to sell it online, highlights the politeness and communal spirit that cricket embodies.

Depending on the stadium, a ball can sometimes be lost. It may end up in the parking lot, water, or thick grass. Training ball-seeking dogs to hunt for it is not worth the effort. To maintain fairness, the umpire retrieves a replacement ball from a box containing 6 to 12 used balls in varying conditions. Umpires regularly inspect the game balls and use their expertise to select one that is closest in condition to the lost ball. Play then continues with the "new" used ball.

Reading the Pitch and Weather: Mastering the Elements

Understanding the pitch and weather conditions is critical for any bowler aiming to outsmart batters. These factors significantly influence the behavior of the ball and must be considered when crafting a bowling strategy. Successfully reading these variables combines keen observation with experience and plays a pivotal role in a bowler's effectiveness.

The Pitch: Types and Characteristics

Pitches can be broadly classified based on their surface characteristics:

- **Green Pitch**: Identified by significant grass cover, these pitches favor fast bowlers by offering seam movement. The moisture content helps the ball deviate off the seam, posing challenges for batters.

- **Dry Pitch**: Lacking grass and often hard, these pitches initially favor batters. However, as the match progresses, they can develop cracks, making them unpredictable and turning into a haven for spinners.

- **Dusty Pitch**: Common in subcontinental conditions, these surfaces suit spinners from the outset. The loose texture allows the ball to grip and turn sharply, complicating life for batters.

Bowlers carefully inspect the pitch before the game and monitor its evolution as the match progresses. Key observations include:

- **Color and Texture**: A greenish tinge suggests seam-friendly conditions, while a brownish, dusty appearance points to spin-favoring surfaces.
- **Hardness**: Testing the surface with a finger or observing warm-up bounces reveals its hardness. Hard pitches yield more bounce and pace, whereas softer pitches slow the ball down.
- **Moisture Content**: Morning dew or recent rain provides moisture that benefits seamers early on but could dry out later, favoring batters.

The Weather's Influence

Weather is an equally decisive factor in cricket. Fast bowlers thrive on overcast days, as the conditions amplify swing and seam movement. Conversely, hot and dry weather is a boon for spinners, aiding turn and bounce. Captains must weigh weather conditions carefully when deciding whether to bat or bowl first.

Key weather factors include:

- **Wind Speed and Direction**: These elements influence a bowler's control and can assist in swinging the ball.
- **Moisture Levels**: A damp field slows the ball's progress toward the boundary, benefiting both bowlers and fielders. In these conditions, captains might opt to bowl first, anticipating that the grass will dry out and enhance their batting prospects in the second innings.

Adapting Strategies to Conditions

Bowling strategies must be tailored to both the pitch and the prevailing weather:

- **Fast Bowlers**: On green pitches, seam and swing deliveries become critical. On hard surfaces, short-pitched balls and bouncers prove more effective.

- **Spin Bowlers**: Dry or dusty pitches allow spinners to vary their pace and use rough patches to generate sharp turns, keeping batters guessing.

- **General Variation**: Regardless of conditions, altering speed, length, and angles adds unpredictability, exploiting the batter's hesitation.

The Evolving Pitch

A cricket pitch is dynamic, changing throughout the match. Footmarks left by runners often become a tool for spinners, providing areas to create more turn. Similarly, worn pitches offer fast bowlers variable bounce and pace. By staying attuned to these developments, bowlers can maintain an edge over batters.

The Bowler's Role and Overs

In T20 cricket, each match consists of 20 overs, with each over containing six legal deliveries. Overs are somewhat analogous to innings in baseball. The desired outcome of a delivery is either a wicket (out) or no runs scored. A delivery that results in no runs is known as a **dot ball**.

The captain decides who will bowl the next over, and the bowler runs up to deliver at least six balls. Each bowler is permitted to bowl only four of the 20 overs, allowing them to showcase their skills through approximately 24 deliveries. If an illegal delivery occurs, such as a **wide** (out of the batter's reach) or a **no-ball** (when the bowler oversteps their mark or delivers the ball directly at the batter's upper body), the bowler must bowl an additional ball. In the case of a no-ball, the batter also receives a **free hit** on the following delivery.

Umpires oversee every delivery, including hits and catches. If a bowler believes they have taken a wicket but the field umpire does not call it, they can try to persuade their captain to use one the team's limited review appeals.

The captain can make real-time adjustments at the end of each over based on the match's circumstances. Matches typically begin with fast bowlers skilled at delivering a shiny, new ball. As the ball is used, it becomes marked and softer, altering its behavior. A common strategy is to assign the fastest bowler to the first and third overs, allowing them to rest in the field until the last two overs, when batters tend to take risks to boost their scores. The second-fastest bowler usually bowls the second and fourth overs. By this time, the ball is worn in, and ideally, one or two batters have been dismissed, allowing spin bowlers to take over during the middle overs.

In the event of a tie at the end of the two innings, a Super Over is played. The team that just finished batting goes first, selecting their best batter, even if they have already been dismissed. The bowling team chooses one of their bowlers to bowl, regardless of whether they have already bowled their four overs. The team that scores the most runs during the Super Over wins the match. If the score is still tied after the first Super Over, another one is played with a different bowler and batter. What is more exciting than overtime in sports?

Mastering Bowling Lines and Lengths

A bowler's success often hinges on two key variables: **Line** and **Length**. These factors determine the trajectory and bounce of the ball, respectively, and are central to outsmarting the batter.

Line: The Direction of the Ball

The **Line** refers to the direction of the ball relative to an imaginary line running straight down between the wickets. Different lines create distinct challenges for the batter:

- **Middle Stump Line (Straight Line):** The ball targets the middle stump, limiting the batter's ability to play shots to either side. This line is highly effective for potential **LBW** (Leg Before Wicket) or **stumped** dismissals.

- **Off Stump Line:** Directed at the off stump (to a right-handed batter's left from the bowler's perspective), this line pressures the batter to protect their stumps while limiting scoring opportunities.

- **Leg Stump Line:** Aimed at the leg stump (to a right-handed batter's right from the bowler's perspective), it can catch the batter off guard while being tricky to score from.

- **Outside Off Stump Line:** Positioned farther to the off side of the off stump, this line tempts batters to play risky shots, especially drives.

- **Outside Leg Stump Line:** Farther to the leg side of the leg stump, this line is often used to frustrate batters or prevent easy runs.

Length: The Ball's Bounce Point

The **Length** describes how far the ball bounces from the batter, impacting both shot selection and dismissal potential. Here are the common lengths:

- **Yorker:** Bouncing within 7 feet of the batter, yorkers target the feet and are tough to defend. They are particularly dangerous, often leading to **LBW** or **bowled** dismissals.

- **Full Pitched Ball:** Landing 7-13 feet away, it arrives around knee height, encouraging powerful drives but still posing a risk for **LBW** or being bowled out.

- **Good Length Ball:** Bouncing 13-26 feet from the batter, this length lands between knee height and the top of the stumps. It leaves the batter uncertain whether to play forward or back, increasing dismissal chances.

- **Short Pitched Ball:** Bouncing over 26 feet away, it reaches chest height. While ineffective for **LBW** or bowled dismissals, it disrupts the batter's rhythm, akin to a brushback pitch in baseball.

- **Bouncer:** Aimed directly at the batter's upper body, bouncers are controversial deliveries. They gained notoriety during the 1932-1933 Ashes series (the "Bodyline" series), leading to debates over the spirit of the game. Today, bouncers are restricted to one per over in T20 cricket.

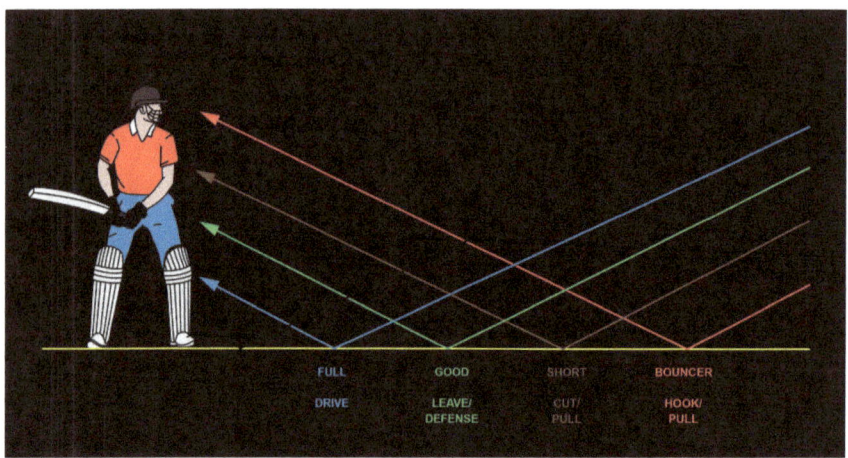

Deception: A Bowler's Weapon

Beyond line and length, bowlers employ wrist motion, grip variations, and spin to confound batters. The batter must carefully watch every delivery, making it crucial for the bowler to disguise their intentions and keep the batter guessing.

Bowling Strategies: Outsmarting the Batter

Strategy is as crucial as raw skill for bowlers aiming to prevent runs and secure wickets. A bowler may possess an exceptional googly, blistering speed, or pinpoint control, but batters are quick to adapt, turning these strengths into potential liabilities. To stay ahead, bowlers must continuously vary their line, length, speed, and spin to deliver balls that confound batters' expectations. This responsibility extends beyond the bowler; captains play a vital role in orchestrating the order of bowlers for maximum impact. This blend of tactical science and artistic intuition shapes the game's strategic depth.

The Death Overs: High Stakes and Precision

The final four to five overs (16-20) of an innings are often referred to as the **Death Overs**, where the intensity of the game reaches its peak. In the first innings, batters aim to post an imposing total, while in the second innings, they look to chase down or surpass the opponent's score. Falling behind on the required run rate forces batters into more aggressive play, increasing their risk-taking. Bowlers must adapt their strategies in real time, balancing containment and wicket-taking based on the match situation and the number of batters remaining.

Fast bowlers often step up during the Death Overs, delivering their final two overs with the primary aim of limiting runs. Counterintuitively, they may reduce their speed, as faster deliveries can travel farther off the bat. Instead, they focus on techniques like **Yorkers**, bouncing the ball near the batter's feet to make full shots difficult. Additionally, fast bowlers widen their line to tempt batters into reaching for off-balance shots, increasing the chance of mistakes.

Golden Ducks and Aggression After Wickets

Every bowler dreams of claiming a **Golden Duck**, dismissing a batter on their very first ball. Following a wicket, bowlers often adopt their most aggressive tactics against a new batter, who may be nervous or overly confident and has yet to establish their rhythm. This momentary vulnerability makes wicket-taking contagious, with dismissals often occurring in clusters.

Enticing the Batter

Bowlers employ clever tactics to lure batters out of their crease. By delivering a ball that appears tempting yet deceptive, they hope the batter misses, allowing the wicketkeeper to catch the ball and break the stumps before the batter can return to safety.

Bowling Styles and Techniques

Cricket bowlers must deliver the ball with a straight arm. While a slight extension is permitted, the arm must not straighten to the extent that it is considered "throwing." Within this restriction, bowlers employ a variety of techniques and styles that define their approach.

Fast/Pace Bowlers

Fast bowlers, also known as **pacers**, deliver the ball at remarkable speeds. They position themselves well behind the crease and take long run-ups—sometimes up to 25 paces or 75 feet. This approach, known as the **Delivery Stride**, generates immense power. Pacers can be classified into two categories:

- **Fast Bowlers:** Bowl consistently between 87–93 mph for men, with the fastest recorded speed reaching around 100 mph. For women, the range is 68–75 mph, with a top record of 82 mph.

- **Medium Fast Bowlers:** Operate at slightly lower speeds but focus on precision and swing.

Fast bowlers often use psychological tactics to unsettle batters. For instance, they might **soften up** a batter with back-foot deliveries before switching to front-foot deliveries to catch them off guard. To increase unpredictability, pacers vary the speed of their deliveries while maintaining consistent run-ups. Subtle grip adjustments, such as spreading the fingers wider, allow for slower deliveries without altering visible technique.

The seam is another key weapon in a pacer's arsenal. By aiming the ball to land on the seam, fast bowlers create unpredictable bounce, further challenging the batter. Additionally, swing bowlers leverage wrist action and seam orientation to achieve lateral movement through the air.

Fast bowling mirrors baseball dynamics: the faster the delivery, the more power it generates upon contact. However, in situations where runs must be restricted, fast bowlers often reduce speed to make boundaries and sixes harder to achieve, focusing instead on conceding singles.

Swing Bowlers

Swing bowlers, a subset of pacers, specialize in using aerodynamics to alter the ball's trajectory mid-air. By polishing one side of the ball and allowing the other to remain rough, they create an imbalance in airflow. This imbalance causes the ball to "swing" toward the rougher side. Swing deliveries are categorized as:

- **Outswinger:** Curves away from the batter's body and stumps.
- **Inswinger:** Starts wider and curves inward toward the batter and stumps.

As the ball wears during an innings, its swing potential diminishes. However, a well-worn ball can achieve **Reverse Swing**, where the rougher side leads the movement, surprising batters with unexpected deviations.

Spin Bowlers

Spin bowlers, or **spinners**, rely on rotation rather than speed to deceive batters. Delivering at slower speeds (45–66 mph), they use spin to manipulate the ball's trajectory after it bounces, aiming to land it near the bat and the stumps. Precision and deception are central to their technique.

- **Wrist Bowlers (Leg Spinners):** Use wrist motion to generate spin, often delivering a **Leg Break**, where the ball moves from right to left after bouncing. They can also bowl a **Googly**, spinning the ball in the opposite direction to surprise the batter.

- **Finger Spin Bowlers (Off Spinners):** Create spin using their fingers. Right-handed off spinners turn the ball from the batter's off side to leg side, while left-handed finger spinners generate movement toward the batter's front foot. Although finger spin offers better control, it produces less turn compared to wrist spin.

The Grips

Every successful delivery begins with the right grip. Different types of bowlers use tailored grips to achieve their desired outcomes:

- **Fast Bowler Grip:** The index and middle fingers rest along the upright seam, with the thumb providing support from underneath. This grip enables swing in either direction, depending on the seam's orientation during rotation.

- **Off-Spin Bowler Grip:** The seam is positioned horizontally, with the top knuckles of the index and middle fingers spread across it. The ball rests against the ring finger, while the thumb and pinkie are tucked to the side. Spin is generated through wrist and finger rotation.

- **Leg-Spin Bowler Grip:** This grip is similar to that of off-spin, but the bowler flicks the ball with their wrist, causing it to spin from the off side to the leg side of a right-handed batter.

- **Swing Bowler Grip:** A shiny side and a rough side create an aerodynamic imbalance. The seam is angled toward the batter, with the shiny side positioned appropriately to produce outswing or inswing.

- **Reverse Swing Grip:** Older, rougher balls naturally reverse their swing direction. Swing bowlers adjust their grips to leverage this effect.

- **Seam Bowler Grip:** This grip is similar to a fast bowler's grip but focuses on landing the seam upright on the pitch to achieve erratic bounce.

Run-up and Delivery

Fast bowlers typically begin their run-up from a significant distance, building momentum to deliver the ball with maximum speed and power. In contrast, spin bowlers rely on precision and control, requiring only a few steps before delivering the ball.

During warm-ups, bowlers determine their optimal starting position by practicing their run-ups, ensuring their front foot lands on or behind the popping crease for a legal delivery. This preparation is similar to how high jumpers mark their approach. To maintain consistency, bowlers mark their starting spot using a small coin, plastic disc, or by scratching the grass. They repeat this process for both ends of the field, as they may bowl from either end during a match.

When delivering the ball:

- The **front foot** must remain behind the popping crease, either grounded or in the air. If the front foot crosses this line, the delivery is deemed a no-ball, which the umpire signals by extending one arm horizontally.

- The **back foot** must land within the area between the return creases. Any contact with or crossing of the return creases results in a no-ball.

This foot placement rule is analogous to a baseball pitcher who must stay on the pitcher's plate (rubber) when beginning their delivery. By enforcing these rules, umpires ensure fair play and consistency throughout the game.

Strategic Fielder Placement

While the role of fielders merits its own chapter, understanding their positioning is essential for grasping the bowler's strategy. The bowler and the team captain collaborate to determine the placement of fielders for each delivery. This process is both an art and a science, blending the captain's overarching strategy with the bowler's intimate understanding of the next ball's trajectory.

Fielder placement relies on educated predictions of where the ball is likely to travel. These decisions take into account the bowler's delivery plan and the batter's tendencies. Adjustments are made dynamically throughout the game, as each delivery influences the batter's responses and the captain's fielding choices.

For example:

- When a bowler prepares to deliver a short-pitched ball, fielders are positioned deeper in the outfield to anticipate potential catches.
- Conversely, for a full-length ball, fielders are placed closer to the batter to prevent quick singles or capitalize on mistakes.

This ongoing coordination between the captain, bowler, and fielders exemplifies the strategic complexity of cricket, adapting continuously as the game unfolds.

Rules Every Bowler Must Know

1. **Pitch Protection**: Bowlers are prohibited from intentionally damaging the pitch. Maintaining the integrity of the playing surface ensures a fair contest for both teams.

2. **Injury Substitutions**: If a bowler is injured mid-over, they can be replaced by another bowler, provided the substitute:

    a. Has not yet completed their four-over limit.

    b. Did not bowl the previous over. The substitute bowler cannot bowl the very next over but may complete the injured bowler's remaining deliveries within the four-over restriction. After treatment, the injured bowler must sit out at least one over before rejoining the game.

3. **Legal Delivery Rules**:

    a. **Full Tosses**: Bowlers can deliver the ball directly to the batter without it bouncing on the ground, known as a **Full Toss** or **In The Full**. For it to be legal, the ball must not pass above the batter's waist when they are in their normal stance. If it does, it is deemed a **no-ball** due to safety concerns, awarding one run to the batting team and granting the batter a **Free Hit**.

    b. No-balls for Height: Any delivery that passes above the batter's head upon arrival is automatically considered a no-ball, resulting in the same penalty as a waist-high full toss.

Getting a Batter Out: Key Dismissals

Bowlers use various techniques to dismiss batters. Below are the most effective and commonly employed methods for achieving a wicket:

- **Caught**: The batter hits the ball into the air, and a fielder catches it before it touches the ground. This is one of the simplest and most frequent forms of dismissal.

- **Bowled**: If the batter misses the ball and it strikes the stumps, dislodging the bails, they are bowled out.

- **Leg Before Wicket (LBW)**: If the ball hits the batter's leg pads and the umpire determines it would have gone on to hit the stumps (had the batter's leg not been in the way), the batter is out. LBW dismissals often require careful umpiring and are frequently reviewed for accuracy.

- **Caught Behind**: If the batter edges the ball with the bat and it is caught by the wicketkeeper, this results in a dismissal. This often occurs when the bowler uses subtle swing or seam movement to deceive the batter.

- **Stumped**: When a batter steps out of the crease to play a shot and misses the ball, the wicketkeeper can catch it and break the stumps before the batter returns to safety. This dismissal is a hallmark of clever spin bowling.

- **Heroic or Lucky Bowler**: Occasionally, extraordinary or fortunate moments lead to dismissals. For instance, a bowler in a vulnerable position after delivering the ball may face a direct hit from the batter at speeds of up to 100 mph. Despite wearing no helmets for protection, bowlers often attempt to catch such shots for a dismissal. Remarkably, there have been instances where the ball, after striking the bowler's shoe, has rebounded unexpectedly to hit the stumps, dismissing the non-striker who was out of the crease.

Decoding Bowling Statistics

Bowling performance is measured through a range of statistics that evaluate a bowler's impact on the game. Below are the key metrics used to determine a bowler's effectiveness:

Runs Per Over (RPO)/Economy Rate

- **Formula**: Total runs conceded ÷ Number of overs bowled.
- **Interpretation**:
  - Below 5: **Excellent**
  - 5–7: **Good**

- o 7–9: **Acceptable**
- o Over 9: **Less favorable**. If a bowler takes wickets, a higher RPO may still be deemed acceptable due to their contributions in dismissing batters. This metric is applicable in individual games, seasons, and career assessments.

Wickets

This metric tracks the number of batters dismissed during a match.

- Taking **1 wicket** is commendable.
- Taking **multiple wickets** is considered excellent. Even without wickets, maintaining a low RPO (e.g., 3) is seen as a strong performance.

Maidens

A **maiden over** is achieved when a bowler concedes no runs during an over.

- A w**icket maiden over** occurs when no runs are conceded, and at least one wicket is taken.
- While the term "maiden" remains in use, some consider it outdated and potentially misogynistic; however, it continues to be a standard term in cricket.

Bowling Average

- **Formula**: Total runs conceded ÷ Total wickets taken.
- **Purpose**: This statistic reflects a bowler's overall performance over a season or career. Lower averages indicate higher effectiveness.

Strike Rate

- **Formula**: Average number of balls bowled per wicket taken.

- **Application**: A lower strike rate demonstrates a bowler's ability to take wickets more frequently, highlighting their impact on the game.

Extras: When Bowling Goes Beyond the Basics

Extras refer to runs awarded to the batting team that are not credited to any individual batter. These runs result from errors or infractions by the fielding team and can significantly influence the game's outcome. Below are the main types of extras:

Wide

- A **wide** delivery is called when the bowler delivers the ball too far for the batter to reasonably hit.

- If the batter steps out and successfully hits a wide delivery, the runs scored are counted as normal, and no extra run is awarded to the batting side.

- If the ball passes without being hit, the batting side is awarded one extra run, and the bowler must deliver a replacement ball, extending the over to seven deliveries.

- Wides count against the bowler but are not credited to the batter. They are judged based on the batter's position; if the batter steps forward and the ball is within their range, it is not considered a wide.

No-Ball

- A **no-ball** is called when the bowler oversteps the popping crease before releasing the ball or violates other delivery rules.

- The batting team is awarded one extra run, which counts against the bowler.

- Additionally, the next delivery becomes a **Free Hit**, giving the batter a chance to swing freely without the risk of being dismissed by a catch or bowled out (although run-outs still apply).

- Any runs scored on a Free Hit are added to the batter's total and counted against the bowler.

Bye

- A bye occurs when the ball passes the batter without contact and evades the wicketkeeper, allowing the batters to run.
- Runs scored, including boundaries, are added to the team's total but do not count against the bowler or toward the batter's individual score.

Leg Bye

- Similar to a bye, a leg bye is awarded when the ball deflects off the batter's body or protective gear and moves away from the wicketkeeper.
- The batters can run if they believe they can score. These runs are added to the team's total but are not credited to the batter or counted against the bowler.
- Leg byes are only granted if the batter was attempting a shot or avoiding the ball. Otherwise, the ball is considered dead, and no runs are scored.

Chapter Five

Fielding: The Unsung Heroes of Cricket

"Catches win matches"—a phrase that encapsulates the vital role fielding plays in cricket. Fielding is a finely honed skill that takes time to appreciate fully. When a ball is hit directly to a fielder for what appears to be an effortless catch, it's easy to assume the player was simply in the right place at the right time. What often goes unnoticed, however, is the intricate strategy involved: bowlers consulting with the captain before the delivery and captains meticulously repositioning fielders to set the perfect trap.

Cricket fielding shares similarities with baseball, as players catch or retrieve the ball to create exciting plays. However, cricket fielding stands apart due to its larger scope—fielders must cover the entire 360 degrees of the playing field, rather than just the 180 degrees in front of the batter, as in baseball. This expansive area demands careful positioning by the captain, whose tactical decisions are pivotal in converting opportunities into success. The larger playing field and dynamic arrangements make cricket fielding a unique and indispensable component of the game.

Although fielding lacks the immediate glamour of batting or bowling, it is a crucial skill that every player must master. Dropping a catch in front of both teams and the crowd is more than just a physical mistake; it can weigh heavily on a player's mind. Fielders often experience psychological pressure, knowing that their error has allowed the batter to continue scoring runs. Additionally, missed catches can have a broader impact on the game, altering the course of an innings and affecting the bowler's statistics by denying them a well-deserved wicket. These moments require both physical execution and mental resilience, as fielders must quickly recover from mistakes to refocus on the game.

The fielding team's arrangement is highly dynamic, constantly shifting to meet the game's demands. In fact, the captain may make as many as six fielding adjustments within a single over.

Captains must account for various factors when directing their players:

- **Bowler's Strategy**: Will the next ball be fast, spin, or swing? Is the bowler left- or right-handed?

- **Batter's Tendencies**: Captains analyze the batter's strengths and weaknesses, often using game footage to predict their behavior. Field placements vary for left- and right-handed batters.

- **Match Situations**: The captain must prioritize between limiting runs and taking wickets. Are the batters required to play aggressively, or can they afford to be patient? Is a new batter at the crease? What is the status of the batting partnership? Is the team still in the power play, which restricts fielders outside the circle?

- **Pitch and Field Conditions**: The pitch influences how the ball behaves, while field conditions determine its speed. A dry field allows the ball to run quickly, while a wet field slows it down.

- **Player Fitness and Skills**: Each player has unique strengths and limitations. Injuries may restrict mobility, influencing their placement on the field.

The fielding team's objectives are twofold: limit the number of runs and dismiss the batters. The emphasis on these goals shifts depending on the situation. Cricket employs both offensive and defensive field placements, with all players except the bowler and wicketkeeper classified as fielders. Fielders are highly vocal, encouraging one another and celebrating exceptional plays. Their excitement reaches a crescendo when they believe a batter is out, creating noise to sway the umpire's decision.

Supporting the team behind the scenes is the twelfth player. This crucial role ensures injured teammates are replaced promptly and that players remain hydrated and equipped throughout the match.

The Cricket Field: Areas and Boundaries

We refer to the cricket field as the **Cricket Oval**, but it can take on various shapes. It typically appears round or somewhat oval, resulting in some parts of the boundary being closer to the batter than others. The field encompasses the entire playing area, including the pitch, infield, and outfield.

The boundary is the edge of the field where runs are scored when the ball reaches or crosses it, and it is marked by a rope, fence, or line. In professional games, boundary advertising wedges are often used to delineate the boundary line while displaying important advertisements, helping us recognize the event's sponsors.

The size and shape of the boundary can vary significantly from event to event. In women's cricket, the boundary is adjusted to account for the physiological differences between male and female athletes while ensuring the excitement and competitiveness of the game are maintained. In men's cricket, the boundary typically has a diameter of 450-500 feet, while in women's cricket, it usually measures 360-420 feet in diameter.

The infield is the area surrounding the pitch and features a 30-yard circle. Close fielders are positioned inside this circle, allowing them to stop the ball before it reaches the outfield, thus preventing runs. They may dive in front of the ball to keep it in the infield, enabling other fielders to retrieve it.

The outfield extends beyond the infield circle to the boundary. Fielders positioned far out are responsible for catching the ball, stopping it from reaching the boundary, and, if successful, throwing it back quickly to run out a batter or end the play.

The wicketkeeper plays a role similar to that of a baseball catcher. They communicate discreetly with the bowler and have a keen sense of where the ball is likely to go. The wicketkeeper must stop any balls that pass the batter before they reach the outfield and closely monitor the batter for any chance to stump them if they stray too far from the popping crease. Additionally, when a ball is fielded, the wicketkeeper is ideally positioned to catch it and knock over the stumps for a run out.

The pitch is the central area on the field where bowlers and batters showcase their skills. Almost all aspects of the pitch are rigidly defined in the Laws of Cricket. It measures 22 yards in length between the stumps at both ends and is 10 feet wide.

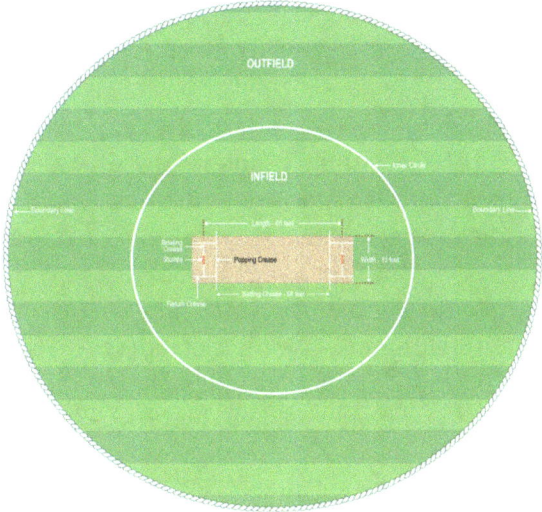

The crease at each end of the pitch is aligned with the stumps and measures 8 feet 8 inches long.

The popping crease is positioned 4 feet in front of, and parallel to, the bowling crease, extending indefinitely on both sides of the pitch. This is where the front foot of the bowler must land during delivery.

The return creases are the two lines perpendicular to both the bowling crease and the popping crease, extending 4 feet 4 inches behind the bowling crease. This is where the back foot must land during delivery.

Understanding Fielding Restrictions

The cricket **circle**, also known as the **30-yard circle**, plays a crucial role in the sport by delineating the infield and enforcing fielding restrictions. Positioned 30 yards from the center of the pitch, this circle regulates the placement of fielders, encouraging aggressive batting by creating gaps in the field, which facilitates boundary scoring. The cricket circle fosters a balanced contest between bat and ball, promoting strategic field placements and dynamic gameplay.

During the **Powerplay Overs** (overs 1–6), fielding restrictions allow only two fielders to be positioned outside the 30-yard circle. This setup gives batters a significant advantage, often resulting in higher scoring opportunities as gaps in the outfield become more accessible.

After the Powerplay, during the **Middle Overs** (7–15) and the **Death Overs** (16–20), a maximum of five fielders are allowed outside the 30-yard circle. This adjustment provides the fielding team with greater flexibility to defend against aggressive batting while attempting to limit runs.

The bowling side must start the 20th over by the 85th minute of the game. If they fail to do so, as a penalty one of the fielders must return to the Circle for the remainder of the match.

No more than two fielders are permitted behind square on the leg side at any time during the game.

Fielding Positions and Their Importance

Cricket differs from baseball in that fielding positions refer to specific locations on the field rather than individual players. Each position has a designated name, and the accompanying graphic provides a complete list along with illustrations of their respective locations. While it's helpful to know the names of these positions, it's not essential to spend time memorizing them.

- **Slip** is positioned next to the wicketkeeper to catch balls that may have edged off the bat.

- **Gully** is wider than slip and also looks for edge shots.

- **Point** is square on the off side.

- **Cover** is located between point and mid-off, primarily for drives.

- **Mid-Off** and **Mid-On** are close to the bowler, ready to catch balls hit straight back in their direction.

- **Mid-Wicket** is positioned on the leg side for pull shots.

- **Fine Leg** is behind the batter to catch glancing shots directed towards the leg side.

- **Third Man** is deep on the off side.

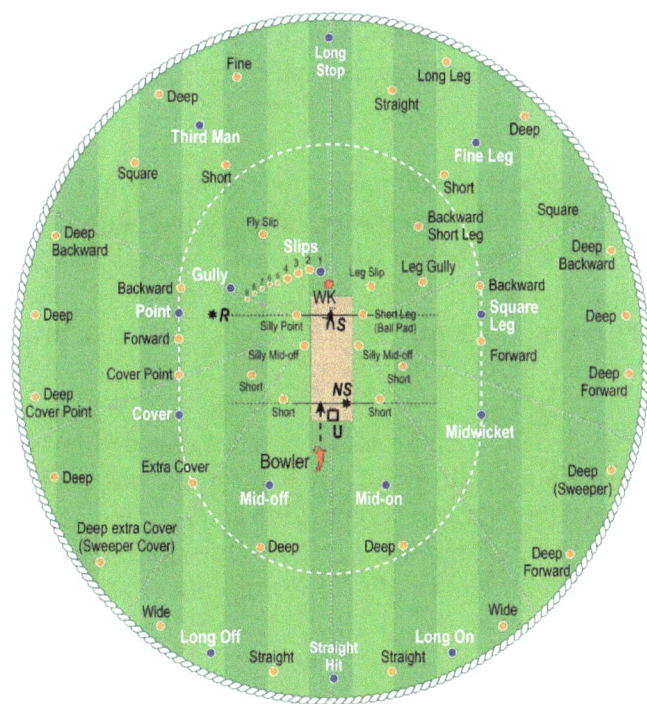

Strategies for Effective Fielding

To minimize runs and secure dismissals, the captain employs a mix of offensive and defensive fielding strategies, carefully adapting to the evolving match situation.

Offensive Fielding: This approach prioritizes taking wickets and is particularly useful for ending the game, dismissing a specific batter, breaking a strong partnership, or maintaining a low run rate against powerful batting teams. Fielders are positioned closer to the batter, allowing them to respond quickly to edges and other chances, converting opportunities into outs with precision.

Defensive Fielding: Defensive fielding focuses on restricting runs, boundaries, and sixes, shifting the priority away from dismissing batters. Fielders are placed deeper in the infield to intercept balls before they reach the outfield, while outfielders are stationed near the boundary to prevent scoring opportunities. This strategy is often employed when the fielding team needs to stifle the batting side's momentum.

The Wicketkeeper's Role: The wicketkeeper's positioning is tailored to the type of bowler and their personal preference. Against fast bowlers, they typically **Stand Back**, several feet behind the stumps, to allow more reaction time for potential catches. This distance also enables some wicketkeepers to remove their helmets and maintain an unobstructed view.

In contrast, when facing spin or slower-paced bowlers, the wicketkeeper moves closer to the stumps, a position known as **Standing Up**. Here, they are prepared to catch deflections off the bat or stray balls and to attempt stumpings. Due to the increased risk of the ball striking them in this position, they wear helmets for protection.

Mastering the Art of Catching

Catching is an art that requires precision, technique, and coordination. Except for the wicketkeeper, fielders must catch the ball barehanded—a challenge that often leads to spectacular plays. However, catches are rarely straightforward; the ball may drop sooner, soar higher, or land awkwardly in the fielder's hands. Whether standing still or sprinting to make a diving catch, fielders must quickly adjust to the ball's unpredictable trajectory. Of course, part of the fun for spectators is confidently declaring, "I would have made that catch!"

When a batter hits the ball and a fielder catches it successfully, the batter is **Caught Out**. If the wicketkeeper makes the catch, the dismissal is known as **Caught Behind**.

Types of Catches

High Catches: High catches require fielders to leap and reach above their heads. To execute these catches effectively, players use the **reverse cup technique**, positioning their fingers upward and aligning their palms to meet the ball.

Low Catches: Low catches are taken below the waist and require the **orthodox cup technique**. In this method, the fingers point downward while the palms face upward, forming a secure cup to cradle the ball.

Slip Catches: Slip catches are made by fielders positioned close to the wicketkeeper. These catches demand exceptional reflexes and "soft hands" to absorb the ball's impact without fumbling it.

Communication and Priority

When multiple fielders converge on a ball, clear communication is vital to prevent collisions and ensure a safe catch. Typically, the fielder closest to the ball and with the best chance of securing it takes priority. This fielder signals their intent by yelling "Mine" or "Got

It," helping to avoid confusion among teammates.

A hierarchy determines priority for catching the ball:

- **Wicketkeeper**: As the closest player to the stumps, the wicketkeeper has the highest priority, especially for edges and top edges.
- **Captain**: If the captain is in a favorable position to catch the ball, they may assert priority.
- **Outfield Coordination**: In the outfield, the fielder running inward toward the ball typically takes precedence over one running outward.

Throwing with Accuracy and Precision

Fielders must master the art of throwing with both power and precision to return the ball effectively to the wicketkeeper, infielder, bowler, or stumps. Whether aiming for a direct hit to secure a thrilling runout or preventing additional runs, their throwing technique can significantly influence the outcome of the match.

Techniques for Effective Throws

Overhand Throws: For long-distance throws, fielders rely on the overhand technique, similar to baseball. This method requires proper foot placement, shoulder rotation, and a strong follow-through, ensuring that the ball travels quickly and accurately to its target. A well-executed overhand throw can prevent a boundary or dismiss a batter attempting a risky run.

Underhand Throws: When fielders are closer to their target, the underhand throw becomes their preferred technique. This method prioritizes control and accuracy, especially in tight situations where precision is more important than speed. Short, controlled throws are ideal for relaying the ball to the wicketkeeper or bowler during close runout opportunities.

Relay Throws: Relay throws involve teamwork and coordination, allowing multiple fielders to cover large distances quickly. For instance, when the ball is deep in the outfield, the fielder closest to the boundary relays it to an intermediary fielder positioned nearer to the infield, who then transfers it to the wicketkeeper or bowler. This method ensures both speed and accuracy in situations where a single throw might fall short.

One-Bounce Throws: Fielders sometimes employ a controlled one-bounce throw to ensure the ball remains catchable while maintaining its speed. This technique is particularly effective when throwing to the wicketkeeper or bowler under pressure, minimizing the risk of an errant throw.

Fielding Communication

Effective communication is crucial for coordinating throws among fielders. Players must quickly decide whether to attempt a direct throw, pass to a teammate, or aim for the stumps. Clear signals ensure seamless transitions and prevent confusion during high-pressure plays.

High-Pressure Scenarios

Accurate throwing becomes especially critical in match-defining moments, such as:

- **Direct Hits for Runouts**: When a batter attempts a risky run, an accurate throw aimed directly at the stumps can secure a runout and shift the game's momentum.

- **Boundary Prevention**: Fielders can prevent boundaries by intercepting the ball near the boundary line. By using speed and athleticism to keep the ball in play, they can limit runs. A quick and precise throw ensures the ball is returned to the infield promptly, minimizing additional runs.

- **Last-Minute Relay Throws**: Coordinated relay throws between fielders allow them to cover large distances quickly and maintain control during high-pressure plays. These throws are particularly valuable when the ball is hit deep into the outfield, ensuring the batting side's scoring opportunities are minimized.

Stopping The Ball: Saving Runs

Fielders often prioritize minimizing runs when a catch is unlikely, focusing on blocking the ball with their hands or bodies to prevent it from reaching the boundary. This crucial action, known as **Fielding the Ball** or simply a **Stop**, showcases the skill and athleticism required for effective fielding. Typically, the ball lands close to the fielder, who must quickly transition from diving or jumping to blocking, retrieving it, and throwing it back to the bowler or wicketkeeper. This sequence demands speed, precision, and teamwork, as fielders may also rely on nearby teammates to assist in relaying the ball. Meanwhile, batters carefully assess the situation to decide whether to attempt additional runs.

Fielders can use any part of their body to stop the ball, especially when it's racing toward the boundary. Stretching out or diving at full length, they often intercept the ball just in time to prevent four runs. In some cases, the fielder deflects the ball to a teammate running in to assist. It's important to note that if a fielder touches the boundary while in contact with the ball, it is automatically counted as a boundary, granting four runs to the batting side.

Preventing six runs is the ultimate defensive priority for the fielding team. To save a six, the ball must not touch the ground before crossing the boundary. If a fielder catches the ball but steps on or touches the boundary in the process, the shot is ruled a six. Interestingly, players are allowed to step over the boundary and return to the field, offering creative options for saving runs.

When the ball is headed over the boundary, fielders have several strategies to stop it:

- They can reach over the boundary to catch the ball, securing an out.

- Alternatively, they can deflect the ball back into the field to prevent a six.

- Some of the most thrilling plays occur when a fielder leaps over the boundary, catches or deflects the ball midair, and tosses it back into the field before landing.

- In exceptional cases, a fielder may leap over the boundary to intercept the ball midair, either deflecting it or catching it and tossing it back into play. The fielder can then land outside the boundary and swiftly re-enter the field to complete the catch.

When teammates are nearby, collaboration creates even more exciting possibilities. For example, one fielder may deflect the ball toward another, who completes the catch for an out, combining athleticism and teamwork into a moment of brilliance.

Backing Up and Recovering Missed Opportunities

Fielding is a team effort that demands constant vigilance and collaboration. Every player must be ready to respond to missed plays, whether it involves backing up for missed catches or recovering from dropped opportunities. Quick thinking and teamwork are crucial for maintaining a strong defense and minimizing extra runs.

- **Backing Up Missed Plays**: Fielders positioned near the bowler or wicketkeeper play a critical role in intercepting balls that slip past them. Mid-on and mid-off fielders should be prepared to sprint toward the ball to limit the batter's chances of taking additional runs. Similarly, slip fielders, gully, and point must act quickly if a ball bypasses the wicketkeeper, while fine leg and third man are instrumental in intercepting deflections heading toward the boundary.

- **Recovering Dropped Catches**: Missed catches are an inevitable part of cricket, but swift recovery can make all the difference. Slip fielders should communicate effectively within the cordon to avoid collisions and be prepared to retrieve dropped chances promptly. Infielders at positions like cover, mid-wicket, or point must react quickly to intercept dropped catches in their zones, while outfielders need to support one another by recovering high or lofted shots and making strong return throws to regain control of the play.

- **Supporting the Wicketkeeper**: Slip fielders, gully, and point are particularly important in assisting the wicketkeeper. When the ball bypasses the keeper, these fielders must act immediately to stop or catch it. Fine leg and third man fielders are equally vital in intercepting missed catches or deflections heading toward the boundary.

By staying alert, communicating effectively, and working as a cohesive unit, fielders can recover from missed plays and maintain pressure on the batting team.

Common Fielding Error and Their Terms

Errors and Descriptions:

- **Dropped Catch**: A fielder fails to catch a ball that should have been caught cleanly.

- **Misfield**: The fielder does not stop or collect the ball cleanly, allowing additional runs to be scored.

- **Overthrow**: A throw to the wicketkeeper or bowler is missed or not collected cleanly, resulting in extra runs for the batting team.

- **Fumble**: A momentary loss of control by a fielder while attempting to stop or catch the ball.

- **Missed Stumping**: The wicketkeeper fails to stump the batter despite having a clear opportunity.

- **Missed Run-Out**: A failure by a fielder or wicketkeeper to run out a batter when given the chance.

- **Boundary Misjudgment**: Misjudging the ball's trajectory near the boundary, allowing it to reach the boundary for four or six runs.

- **Parry**: When a fielder inadvertently deflects the ball, potentially causing missed catching opportunities or extra runs.

Expressions for Fielding Errors:

- **"They put it down"**: Refers to a dropped catch.

- **"Misfielded"**: Indicates a failure to stop the ball cleanly.

- **"Overthrows"**: Additional runs taken due to a misdirected throw.

- **"Fumbled"**: Describes mishandling of the ball by a fielder.

- **"Let it through"**: Used when a ball passes a fielder without being stopped.

The Laws and Rules of Fielding

Fielding is governed by strict laws designed to ensure fairness and maintain the integrity of the game. These rules cover a wide range of actions and scenarios:

Run-Outs and Stumping: A fielder may throw the ball directly at the wickets to attempt a run-out. If the wickets are missed, other fielders positioned behind the stumps are responsible for retrieving the ball. A batter is considered **run-out** if the wickets are hit while they are running and have not established ground behind the crease. If a wicketkeeper executes a dismissal in a similar scenario while the batter is stationary or off balance, it is termed **stumping.**

Contact with the Ball: Fielders are only allowed to touch the ball with their hands, arms, or body. Using external objects, such as a hat, to field the ball results in the batting team being awarded **five penalty runs.**

Fielding Position: Fielders are not permitted to significantly change their position during the bowler's delivery stride. Any major movement is considered unfair and can lead to the umpire calling a **dead ball.** Minor positional adjustments to anticipate the ball's direction are allowed, provided they do not distract the batter. This rule also applies to the wicketkeeper.

The Dead Ball Rule: The ball is considered **dead** when it is no longer in play. This occurs in several scenarios, such as:

- When the bowler or wicketkeeper has the ball in their hands after a play.
- When a batter is dismissed.
- When a boundary is scored.

During these moments, the game pauses, and no runs or dismissals can occur until the ball is officially back in play. The umpire may also call a dead ball in situations involving player injury or external interference.

Deception and Distraction: Fielders must avoid deceptive actions, such as pretending to throw the ball when they do not have it, or any behavior aimed at distracting the batter or runners. Such actions are prohibited under cricket's laws.

Eligibility for a Catch: The ball remains eligible for a catch even if it deflects off another fielder, a helmet, or other objects, as long as it does not touch the ground.

Helmets and Clothing on the Field: Fielders, including the wicketkeeper, may place their helmets or clothing on the field. However, if the batters attempt a run and the ball hits the helmet or clothing, the batting team is awarded **five penalty runs** in addition to any runs already scored. Despite this risk, wicketkeepers often place their helmets on the ground when facing fast bowlers for better visibility.

Substitute Fielders: If a fielder is injured, they can be replaced by the **twelfth player,** who is allowed to field but cannot bat or bowl. The injured player may re-enter the match once ready but must serve a penalty period based on the duration of their absence before resuming full participation.

Stumping Mechanics: A batter is also considered stumped if they are not grounded when the ball deflects off the wicketkeeper and hits the stumps. Importantly, a fielder may only stump a batter with the hand holding the ball. A batter is declared out as soon as both ends of one bail are dislodged from the stumps.

Chapter Six

Umpires and Signals: Decisions and Communication

Umpires exemplify the best aspects of cricket. Although they may resemble baseball umpires, cricket's deep-rooted history as an English sport and its strict code of conduct set them apart. Player and coach misconduct, common in many other sports, is virtually absent in cricket, where the governing body emphasizes the **spirit of the game** so strongly that regulations are referred to as **laws**, not rules.

Modern technology further upholds the fairness of cricket. The **Decision Review System (DRS)**, comparable to tennis's replay system, provides indisputable evidence for making correct calls. Unlike in many other sports, cricket umpires demonstrate humility, occasionally requesting reviews of their own decisions when uncertain. Interestingly, only one in four calls are overturned, a testament to the system's reliability.

A unique feature of cricket is that umpires do not make calls unless prompted by the players. Unlike baseball umpires, who dramatically declare "strike one" or "ball four," cricket umpires remain composed and observant, waiting for the fielding side to appeal. When the bowler, wicketkeeper, or fielders believe a batter is out, they shout **Howzat** (how's that) or **Howzee** (how's he). This is often accompanied by enthusiastic displays of celebration, with players high-fiving and cheering. However, if the umpire disagrees, they indicate **Not Out** by remaining motionless. This dynamic can confuse spectators, as frequent appeals can make a dismissal seem inevitable, when in reality, the umpire's decision is anything but certain.

After this decision, the fielding team must decide whether to challenge the ruling using one of their limited reviews. Captains have just 15 seconds to make this decision, typically relying on passionate pleas from their bowler or fielder. If they choose to challenge, they indicate this by making a T sign with their hands. Upon a challenge, the on-field umpire signals a square box with their hands, referring the matter to the third umpire to **Check Upstairs**.

The third umpire, seated in an elevated position with access to multiple replays and the **DRS**, reviews the footage to determine whether to uphold or overturn the decision. At some stadiums, the decision is revealed publicly on large video screens, adding to the suspense. The third umpire communicates their findings via microphone, guiding the on-field umpire to either **Stay With** the original call or issue a revised verdict.

Batters can also review dismissal decisions. For example, in the case of a **Leg Before Wicket (LBW)**, they may believe the ball hit their bat before striking their pads, which would mean they are Not Out. Like the fielding team, batters have 15 seconds to request a review, which is initiated by signaling with their hands in the shape of a T. If the batter is the team captain, they make the decision; otherwise, the affected batter decides.

Each side is usually allowed one unsuccessful challenge per innings. However, if the challenge is successful or inconclusive, they retain the right to challenge again. Without DRS, umpires traditionally give the batter the benefit of the doubt in close cases, such as runouts, catches, and LBWs. However, with the technology available, uncertain umpires can now consult the third umpire, ensuring that the final decision is as accurate as possible.

The Role of Umpires: What You Should Know

The two on-field umpires collaborate closely to ensure the game runs smoothly. Each umpire has specific responsibilities based on their position—Striker's End or Bowler's End—but they frequently consult each other to make joint decisions on complex scenarios. Effective communication is crucial, whether confirming an LBW ruling, clarifying a runout, or monitoring crease violations. In the event of a disagreement, the Bowler's End umpire typically has the final say, as they are regarded as the primary decision-maker in most situations. This structure promotes efficient resolution while maintaining fairness and minimizing interruptions to play. Their collaboration is vital to upholding the integrity of cricket's laws.

Responsibilities of the Bowler's End Umpire

The Bowler's End umpire stands with their back to the oncoming bowler, which can appear obstructive. They are responsible for ensuring that the bowler does not overstep the popping crease, as this would result in a no-ball. This umpire also judges Leg Before Wicket (LBW) decisions and runouts while monitoring the fielders to ensure they are in legal positions during and after the Power Play. Additionally, they communicate with the players and verify that the ball is in proper playing condition.

Responsibilities of the Striker's End Umpire

The Striker's End umpire stands directly behind the wicketkeeper, providing a clear view of the crease and the bowler's delivery. They adjust their position slightly based on whether the batters are right- or left-handed to maintain an unobstructed line of sight. The responsibilities of the Striker's End umpire include:

- Calling wides and no-balls
- Making LBW decisions in conjunction with the Bowler's End umpire
- Monitoring Crease Violations
- Signaling reviews
- Overseeing playing conditions
- Managing time restraints
- Assisting the Bowler's End umpire

The Decision Review System (DRS)

The **Decision Review System (DRS)** is far from dull; it injects suspense and precision into cricket matches. Much like Hawkeye® replays in tennis, the DRS captivates both players and fans, creating a thrilling anticipation to see whether the umpire's decision will stand. Despite its technical complexity, the graphics and procedures are highly viewer-friendly, making it an integral part of modern cricket.

How the DRS Works

Consider a scenario where the umpire calls **Not Out**, but the fielding team believes it should have been **Leg Before Wicket (LBW)**. The captain signals for a review by forming a "T" with their hands. The review process unfolds in three key stages:

1. **Initial Check**: The third umpire first confirms that the bowler delivered the ball legally. If the bowler overstepped the crease, it is deemed a **no-ball**, and the batter is automatically **Not Out**. This step is usually a formality.

2. **UltraEdge® Analysis**: Microphones near the stumps capture sound waves during play as the ball hits the bat or pads. A unique sound spike graphically represented on an onscreen graph reveals any contact. By syncing these spikes with a slow-motion replay, the third umpire determines whether the ball struck the bat before hitting the pad. If bat contact is confirmed, the batter remains **Not Out**.

3. **Ball Tracking**: If no bat contact is detected, the third umpire uses Virtual Eye® technology to assess whether the ball would have hit the stumps. This system extrapolates the ball's trajectory indicating whether it would have hit the wicket, missed to the side, or gone over the top. The batter is considered out only if it is determined that the ball would have hit the stumps had it not been obstructed.

Once the third umpire completes the review, they communicate their decision to the on-field umpire, either confirming the original call or suggesting a change. If the evidence is inconclusive, the initial ruling remains in effect, and the team retains the option to review a future decision.

Beyond LBW: Other Uses of DRS

The Decision Review System (DRS) is not limited to LBW decisions; it plays a vital role in ensuring accuracy across various situations:

- **Caught Behinds:** The third umpire is often called upon to determine whether a batter edged the ball before it was caught by the wicketkeeper or a fielder. Using **ultra-edge** or **snickometer** technology, even faint nicks can be identified, ensuring fair decisions.

- **Boundary Catches:** The third umpire reviews boundary catches to verify whether a fielder stepped on or over the boundary line while attempting the catch.

- **Hitting the Bat:** In close calls between bat and pad, the third umpire can confirm whether the ball made contact with the bat or only the pad, which is crucial for dismissals like caught behind or LBW.

- **Grounded Balls:** The third umpire may be consulted to check if the ball hit the ground before being caught, ensuring the dismissal is valid.

- **Boundary Verification:** Rarely, the third umpire reviews whether the ball hit the ground, touched the boundary rope, or cleared it cleanly for a six.

Judging these scenarios in real-time is often challenging, making DRS an indispensable tool for enhancing accuracy and fairness.

Handling Discipline: Penalties and Warnings

Umpires play a crucial role in upholding fair play and maintaining the spirit of cricket. Their authority enables them to take disciplinary actions that range from warnings to more severe penalties, depending on the level of misconduct.

- **Level 1 and 2 Offenses**: Minor offenses, such as dissent, time-wasting, or minor breaches of conduct, may result in warnings or penalty runs awarded to the opposing team.

- **Level 3 Offenses**: More serious offenses, such as showing dissent at an umpire's decision through inappropriate behavior or using obscene language, warrant stricter penalties. Umpires can send players off the field for a specified period as a consequence.

- **Level 4 Offenses**: Severe breaches, including threatening an umpire, physical assault, or other violent conduct, result in the harshest penalties. Umpires have the authority to send a player off the field for the remainder of the match.

Umpires can also submit formal reports of player misconduct, which may lead to additional disciplinary actions by cricket's governing bodies.

One notable incident occurred during a 2024 Test match between India and Australia at the iconic Melbourne Cricket Ground (MCG). India's Virat Kohli collided with Australia's Sam Konstas while crossing the pitch, sparking a heated exchange. As a result, Kohli was fined 20% of his match fee and received one demerit point for inappropriate contact. While such behavior would go unnoticed in other sports, it drew significant press in the cricketing world, highlighting the game's strict adherence to its code of conduct.

Penalty Runs: When Rules Are Broken

Umpires have the authority to award penalty runs to a team when the opposing side breaches the rules. These penalties uphold fairness and discourage misconduct during play.

Penalties Awarded to the Fielding Side

The fielding team may be penalized for actions that disrupt fair play or violate the laws of cricket:

- **Illegal Fielding**: Using external objects, such as a hat, to field the ball.

- **Ball Tampering**: Altering the ball's condition through illegal means.

- **Obstructing the Batter**: Deliberately blocking a batter's run.

- **Excessive Appeals**: Repeatedly appealing decisions to influence the umpire.

- **Deliberate Distraction or Deception**: Intentionally distracting or deceiving the batter during play.

- **Players Leaving the Field**: Fielders exiting the field without the umpire's permission.

- **Throwing the Ball**: Throwing the ball unnecessarily or in a dangerous manner.

Penalties Awarded to the Batting Side

The batting team may incur penalties if they engage in behavior that disrupts play or violates the rules:

- **Batter Obstructing the Field**: Deliberately blocking or hindering a fielder.

- **Batter Returning the Ball**: Throwing the ball back to a fielder without their consent.

- **Player Misconduct**: Offensive behavior or any form of misconduct by batters.

Weather Interruptions: Adjusting Gameplay and Outcomes

As often stated, weather is the enemy of cricket. Umpires are responsible for making all decisions regarding rain delays, with their primary goal being to ensure player safety while maintaining the fairness and integrity of the game.

When rain begins, umpires call for a delay, prompting the grounds staff to quickly cover the pitch. Once the rain stops, umpires assess the playing conditions, including the pitch, outfield, and overall weather. Regular inspections are conducted to determine whether it is safe to resume play.

Constant communication with grounds staff, team captains, and other officials is critical, as wet or slippery conditions can pose serious risks to players. A damaged pitch can unfairly disadvantage one team, while a waterlogged outfield affects the ball's movement and the fielders' ability to perform effectively.

Managing Matches Under Weather Disruptions

Scenario 1: Game Called Before Both Teams Have Completed Five Overs

If neither team has completed at least five overs, the match is declared a **No Result**. For example, if rain interrupts play during the fourth over of the second innings, the game ends without a result.

Scenario 2: Delayed Start with Reduced Overs

When a significant rain delay prevents the match from starting on time, officials may shorten the game to fit within the available timeframe. For instance, each side might be allotted 10 overs instead of 20. The team batting first aims to maximize their score during these reduced overs, while the second team must chase the target, needing one more run to secure victory.

Scenario 3: Second Innings Halted Midway

If rain causes the game to be **abandoned** during the second innings, the **Duckworth-Lewis-Stern (DLS) method** is used to determine the result. This method ensures fairness by adjusting the target score based on the resources remaining for the chasing team, including overs and wickets.

For example, if Team A scores 201 runs in 20 overs and Team B has completed 10 overs when rain interrupts play, the DLS method will calculate a **Par Score**—the minimum runs Team B needs at that point to be level with Team A. Suppose the par score is 102 runs; if Team B has scored 105, they win. A score of 98 results in a loss, while a score of 102 results in a tie.

The **DLS Par Score** is updated after each ball and displayed on the scoreboard, adding to the tension as both teams adjust their strategies. Dot balls slightly increase the par score, while losing a wicket causes a significant rise, as wickets are a crucial resource in DLS calculations.

Scenario 4: Weather Interrupts the First Innings but Play Continues

If rain interrupts play during the first innings, the umpires may decide to shorten the match. In this case, the **DLS method** is used to calculate a **Target Score** for the second innings. Importantly, the score from the first innings cannot be used as is, since the team batting second would have the advantage of knowing the game is shorter, allowing them to adjust their strategy accordingly. The target score accounts for the reduced number of overs while ensuring a fair chase that reflects both teams' resources.

For example, if the match is reduced to 12 overs per side, the DLS method generates a revised target score based on the runs scored by the first team, the overs remaining, and the number of wickets in hand. This ensures that the team batting second has a fair challenge despite the shortened format.

The **Target Score** remains fixed throughout the second innings, allowing spectators to enjoy a balanced and exciting contest even when weather disrupts the game.

Managing the Cricket Ball: Maintenance and Replacement

The management of the cricket ball is a critical responsibility for umpires, as its condition significantly affects the integrity of the game. Over the course of play, the ball naturally evolves due to wear and tear, impacting its hardness, shine, and performance. To ensure fairness, umpires strive to maintain the ball's consistency. Unlike baseball, where balls are frequently replaced, cricket emphasizes keeping the same ball to preserve gameplay dynamics.

When a ball is hit into the stands, fans typically return it to the nearest fielder, reflecting cricket's unique communal spirit. This practice allows play to continue uninterrupted with the same ball. However, if the ball is hit out of the park, into inaccessible areas, or becomes unfit for play, umpires are responsible for selecting a replacement.

The fielding team can alert the umpires to a lost or damaged ball, but umpires also independently monitor its condition throughout the game. To ensure continuity, umpires carry a box of spare balls, categorized by varying levels of wear and tear. This meticulous system enables them to replace a lost or damaged ball with one that closely matches the condition of the original, ensuring the game remains as fair and consistent as possible.

Key Signals Every Fan Should Know

Out:
The umpire raises one index finger in the air, indicating that the batter is dismissed.

Not Out:
The umpire waves both arms in a sweeping motion in front of their chest, signaling that the batter is not out.

Four Runs:
The umpire waves the right hand horizontally across the body, indicating that the ball has passed the boundary after bouncing once.

Six Runs:
The umpire raises both arms above their head, signaling that the ball has cleared the boundary without bouncing.

DRS or Third Umpire:
The umpire signals a rectangle with both hands, indicating a review or referral to the third umpire under the Decision Review System (DRS).

Wide Ball:
The umpire extends both arms horizontally, signaling that the ball passed out of the batter's reach.

No-ball:
The umpire extends one arm horizontally, indicating that the bowler has delivered an illegal ball.

Free Hit:
The umpire raises one hand above their head and makes a circular motion, which follows certain types of no-ball deliveries.

Bye:
The umpire raises one arm above their head, indicating that the batter has run and scored runs without hitting the ball.

Leg Bye:
The umpire taps a raised knee, signaling that runs are scored when the ball hits the batter's body (except their hands) and they are awarded a run.

Penalty Runs:
The umpire places one hand on their opposite shoulder, awarding extra runs to the batting team due to a rule violation by the fielding team.

Dead Ball:
The umpire crosses and uncrosses both arms in front of their body, signifying that the ball is dead and no further play can occur. The umpire can call a dead ball for various reasons including player injury, pitch obstruction, or external interruptions, such as a bird entering play.

Short Run:
The umpire touches their nearer shoulder with a hand, indicating that the batter didn't complete a run.

End of Powerplay:
The umpire rotates one arm in a large circle above their head.

UNDERSTANDING CRICKET

New Ball:
The umpire points towards the ball with one hand, indicating that a new ball has been taken after a predetermined number of overs.

Revoke Decision:
The umpire puts one hand over the other above their head and then separates them, canceling a previous decision.

Chapter Seven

Exploring Cricket's Other Formats

One fascinating aspect of cricket is its existence in multiple formats, each with slightly different rules and durations. The three main formats of cricket—**T20**, **Test**, and **One Day International (ODI)**—each bring their own distinct style to the sport. While the essence of the game remains consistent, the tactics employed by teams vary significantly depending on the format. For instance, **Test cricket** emphasizes patience and long-term planning, providing a stark contrast to the rapid pace and aggressive play of **T20** cricket, as well as the balanced mix of strategy and speed required in **ODIs**.

A single game is referred to as a **match**, while multiple games within a contest are known as a **series** or **fixtures**. The transitions between formats add an intriguing layer to the game, as players and teams must continually adapt their strategies. In T20s, aggression and quick scoring take center stage, while ODIs require a balanced approach that combines steady run accumulation with bursts of intensity. Test cricket, on the other hand, serves as the ultimate test of endurance, patience, and meticulous planning—challenging players both physically and mentally.

Multi-Format Series: A New Dimension

Increasingly, nations are embracing **multi-format series**, which combine the three main formats into a single competition. These series often feature **three T20 matches**, **two or three ODIs**, and **one Test match**. To determine the overall winner, matches are **weighted by format**, with points awarded for wins, ties, and no results. Test matches typically carry the highest weight due to their length and strategic complexity.

Multi-format series not only provide fans with dynamic competitions but also showcase the versatility of the world's top players. Watching them adapt their skills and strategies across formats adds depth and excitement, making these series a true celebration of the sport.

Beyond the Professional Level

While these professional formats are widely broadcast on TV, cricket's reach extends far beyond organized leagues and tournaments. Children around the world often turn any open space into a makeshift cricket field, embodying the game's universal appeal. On the beaches of the **Caribbean**, spirited games of **beach cricket** reflect the joy and creativity that informal play brings to the sport.

Understanding these diverse formats becomes much easier once you're familiar with the fast-paced **T20 style**. Each format offers its own challenges and thrills, making cricket a sport of endless possibilities for players and fans alike.

Test Cricket: The Pinnacle of Tradition

When you hear the word "cricket," if you picture players dressed in white competing for days with leisurely breaks for tea, you are envisioning **Test** cricket, the most traditional format of the sport. Often referred to as **First-Class** cricket, this format has a rich and complex history that formally began in **1877** and has evolved significantly over time.

A Legacy Passed Down

For fans from cricketing strongholds like **England** and **Australia**— particularly those over 50—Test cricket embodies the essence of the game. It's the format they grew up with, and their passion for it has been passed down through generations. However, younger fans, especially those under 30 or from emerging cricket-playing nations, are more likely to associate the sport with the fast-paced **T20 format**.

While learning about Test cricket is crucial to understanding the game's heritage, new fans—in countries like the United States—will find it easier to start with **T20** and transition into the intricacies of Test matches over time.

The Essence of Test Cricket

Test cricket is a **marathon**, with matches spanning up to **five days**. Unlike the limited-overs formats, each team has **two innings**, and there are no restrictions on the number of overs bowled. It is not unusual to see **150+ overs** in a single innings. This slower, more strategic approach places a premium on skill, stamina, and patience.

Key Features of Test Cricket:

- **White Clothing:** All players wear white uniforms, preserving tradition.
- **Red Ball vs. Pink Ball:** Traditionally played during the day using a **red ball**, which is more visible in sunlight. Day/Night Tests use a **pink ball**, giving rise to the

nickname **red ball cricket**.

- **Unlimited Overs:** An innings continues until ten wickets fall or the batting captain **declares**—a strategic decision to end the innings early in order to maximize the team's chances of achieving a result within the match's time frame.

- **All Batters Get to Play:** Since all **eleven batters** typically get the chance to bat, there is a greater emphasis on bowlers earning wickets.

- **Unlimited Bowler Overs:** Bowlers can deliver as many overs as required, allowing standout bowlers to shine in extended spells.

- **Time Management:** Each day is divided into **three two-hour sessions**, with a **40-minute lunch break** and a **20-minute tea break**.

- **Durability and Patience:** Teams must be prepared for extended batting, bowling, and fielding sessions, requiring both physical and mental endurance.

Test cricket's unique structure opens the door for **complex strategies**. Captains face pivotal decisions, such as when to declare or how to rotate bowlers, to maximize their chances of securing a result within the five-day window.

Strategies and Gameplay

- **The Art of Patience:** Batters often play defensively, **blocking** consecutive balls to wear down bowlers. Bowlers, in turn, rely on subtle variations to outmaneuver batters over time.

- **Declaring:** Captains may declare an innings early, which is a strategic decision to end the innings before all ten wickets fall. This tactic is often employed to ensure there is enough time to dismiss the opposing team and pursue victory within the match's timeframe.

- **The Follow-On:** If the team batting second scores significantly fewer runs in their first innings—trailing by at least **200 runs** in a five-day Test match (with lower margins for shorter matches)—the leading team can enforce the follow-on. This rule requires the trailing team to bat again immediately in their second innings, enabling the leading team to maintain pressure and control of the game.

- **Weather Challenges:** Rain frequently disrupts matches, forcing players off the field and prompting umpires to extend play or abandon the day. In Test cricket, the **Duckworth-Lewis-Stern (DLS) method** is not used to calculate revised targets since there is no fixed number of overs. If a match is not completed within **five days**, it results in a **draw**, regardless of the score.

Unique Features

Unlike T20 or ODIs, Test cricket has:

- **No Powerplays or Bowling Restrictions:** Bowlers can deliver prolonged spells without limitations, emphasizing endurance and strategy.

- **Historic Records:** For instance, in 1997, a Sri Lankan batter scored **340 runs** in a single innings, spending over 13 hours at the crease. His team scored a record-breaking **952 runs**, though most matches feature scores between **280–320** runs per innings.

One of the most remarkable Test matches occurred in 1939, lasting **12 days**, including rest days. Played between **England and South Africa**, the match ended inconclusively because the ship back to England was departing—a rare logistical constraint!

A Different Experience for Fans

Test cricket attracts a unique audience, often comprised of purists who appreciate its **strategic depth** and slower pace. Attending a match requires dedicating an entire day—or even multiple days. While T20 dominates viewership and revenue, Test matches, particularly those between national teams, draw passionate crowds eager to see their countries compete in cricket's most prestigious format.

Test Cricket's Global Prestige

The International Cricket Council (ICC) grants Test cricket privileges exclusively to its **Full Member nations**, a group of twelve countries. **USA Cricket**, as part of its **Foundational Plan**, has set an ambitious goal of achieving ICC Full Membership by **2030**. This includes building ICC-standard venues, increasing grassroots participation, and showcasing enhanced performance from both the men's and women's national teams.

One Day International (ODI): A Day of Action

One Day International (ODI) cricket, pronounced 'O-D-I,' originated in the 1970s as a shorter, action-packed alternative to Test cricket. With matches completed in a single day, this format offers definitive outcomes, making it more accessible for fans who need only one day off work to watch a match. Featuring a limited number of overs, ODIs are characterized by aggressive, high-energy gameplay. For fans looking to expand beyond T20 cricket, ODIs provide an excellent balance of strategy and excitement.

To fit into a single day, ODIs are capped at **50 overs per innings** (300 balls)**,** with each team allotted **3.5 hours** to complete their innings, separated by a **40–45-minute break** for rest and pitch maintenance. Matches typically last around eight hours, though outstanding hitting or bowling can conclude them earlier. Day matches generally start at 9:30 AM, while **day-night matches**, beginning around 2 PM, offer cooler evening conditions and opportunities for fans to attend after work.

127

A Feast of Colors and Strategy

In ODIs, teams wear uniforms in their national colors, creating a vibrant visual spectacle. For example, Australia dons yellow and green, India sports sky blue with orange accents, and the Netherlands captivates with orange and blue. Unlike the timeless white uniforms of Test matches, ODI attire reflects the fun spirit and energy of the game.

ODIs blend the patience of Test cricket with the urgency of T20. The limited overs present strategic challenges:

- **Batting Depth:** The lower-order batters don't always get a chance to bat, emphasizing the need for strong top and middle-order players.

- **Bowling:** Each bowler is restricted to a maximum of **10 overs**, requiring teams to field at least five reliable bowlers while having backups in case of injury or poor performances.

Batting approaches vary depending on the situation. If early wickets fall, batters often play conservatively; if a team retains wickets late into the innings, they can adopt an aggressive, high-scoring strategy.

ODI matches are played with a **white ball**, designed for greater visibility under both daylight and floodlights. This is particularly important for day/night matches, as the white ball contrasts better against darker skies, making it easier for players and fans to track.

Powerplays and Death Overs

ODIs **Powerplays** encourage high-scoring opportunities by restricting the number of fielders outside the 30-yard circle:

- **Overs 1–10 (First Powerplay):** Only two fielders are allowed outside the circle.
- **Overs 11–40 (Middle Overs):** Four fielders are allowed.
- **Overs 41–50 (Death Overs):** Five fielders are allowed in men's matches, while women's matches permit four.

The Death Overs are pivotal, often determining the outcome of the game. Batters take bold risks to maximize runs, while bowlers focus on securing critical wickets. Captains strategically manage their bowlers by deploying their strongest ones early to seize control, while also ensuring they conserve enough overs to unleash these talents during the crucial final moments of the match. These bowlers are expected to perform under intense pressure, using their skill and experience to minimize runs and potentially secure the match with key dismissals.

When the Unexpected Happens

Tied ODIs are resolved through a **Super Over**, where each team gets an additional over to score as many runs as possible. If the tie persists, additional tiebreakers may be employed. For weather interruptions, the **Duckworth-Lewis-Stern (DLS) method** determines a fair result, provided both sides have played at least **20 overs**.

ODI's Crown Jewel: The ICC Cricket World Cup

The **ICC Cricket World Cup**, held every four years, is the premier ODI tournament. Teams qualify based on ICC rankings and performance in qualifying events, with Full Members enjoying automatic privileges. While political factors may influence participation, the tournament guarantees excitement as nations compete for cricketing glory.

USA Cricket: Breaking into ODIs

Both the United States men's and women's cricket teams have varying levels of access to **One Day International (ODI)** matches, depending on their ICC status:

- **U.S. Men's Team:** The U.S. men's cricket team has held **ODI status** since 2019, earning this recognition by excelling in ICC tournaments, particularly during the ICC World Cricket League Division 2. With ODI status, they can compete in official ODI matches and participate in key events like the **ICC Cricket World Cup Qualifiers**.

- **U.S. Women's Team:** Currently, the U.S. women's cricket team does not have ODI status and primarily competes in T20 matches. The women's program in the U.S. is still in its developmental phase. Achieving ODI status for the women's team would require outstanding performance in ICC competitions, as well as meeting specific development benchmarks set by the ICC.

Both teams are actively working to elevate their presence in international cricket. The **USA Cricket Foundational Plan** sets ambitious goals for 2030, which include:

- Building ICC-standard venues.
- Expanding grassroots participation.
- Enhancing the performance of U.S. national teams.

These efforts aim to strengthen U.S. cricket overall and potentially increase opportunities for the women's team to play in ODI matches in the future.

Why Watch ODIs?

ODIs offer a perfect middle ground for fans of Test and T20 cricket. With action-packed gameplay and enough time for strategies to unfold, this format is engaging yet digestible. Whether you're a casual viewer or a die-hard fan, watching the best players from two nations compete for victory is always an exhilarating experience.

One of the highlights of ODIs is the chance to watch your favorite bowlers in action for an extended period. Bowlers are permitted to deliver up to **ten overs** per innings, making it one of the longest continuous spells of bowling in limited-overs cricket. This allows fans to appreciate the skill, endurance, and strategy that bowlers contribute to the game.

The Hundred: Cricket's Perfect Middle Ground

For fans who find T20, Test and ODI formats too lengthy, **The Hundred** offers a well-balanced alternative. Introduced in 2018, this exciting format has quickly gained a dedicated following. T20 players transition seamlessly to The Hundred, allowing fans to watch their favorite cricketers in a fresh context.

As the name suggests, **The Hundred** features only 100 balls per innings, making it shorter than T20's 120 balls. Matches last around **2.5 hours**. This condensed format promotes fast-paced action, characterized by aggressive batting and higher scoring rates, making it ideal for fans seeking non-stop excitement.

Simplified Format

- Each **over** in The Hundred consists of **five balls** instead of the standard **six**.

- A total of **20 overs per innings** maintains a structured pace, with a short break between innings.

- Bowlers can deliver **up to four overs** (20 balls), promoting an aggressive approach as they face fewer batters. Securing early wickets becomes pivotal for gaining the upper hand.

Powerplay and Substitutions

The Hundred incorporates a **Powerplay** during the first 10 balls of an innings, restricting the fielding team to only two fielders outside the 30-yard circle. After this period, two additional fielders may position themselves outside the circle, allowing for better boundary defense.

Unique to this format, teams are permitted to make **tactical substitutions**, replacing players strategically to adapt to evolving match conditions. This innovation adds a layer of complexity and excitement to the game.

Handling Weather Interruptions

Like other formats, The Hundred employs the **Duckworth-Lewis-Stern (DLS) method** to calculate results when weather disrupts play. A minimum of **25 balls** must be bowled in the second innings for a result to be determined.

T10: The Shortest Form of Cricket

The T10 format is the most condensed version of professional cricket, with matches lasting approximately **90 minutes**. Each innings is limited to just **10 overs**, making this format highly dynamic and action-packed. Bowlers are restricted to a maximum of **2 overs** each, and the first **2 overs** of every innings are designated as the **Powerplay**, during which only two fielders can be stationed outside the 30-yard circle.

The brevity of T10 cricket encourages highly aggressive batting, as players prioritize maximizing runs over preserving wickets. This high-stakes approach ensures continuous excitement, with big hits and rapid run chases being common features. As such, T10 serves as a perfect introduction to cricket for new fans while also catering to those seeking quick and thrilling matches.

The T10 format has gained immense popularity in the **Middle East**, with the **Abu Dhabi T10 League** serving as its flagship event. Held annually in the UAE, this league attracts international attention by showcasing some of the world's best players in fast-paced, high-stakes matches. The region's strong interest in cricket, combined with a preference for shorter, action-packed games, has made T10 a favorite among fans. The league's success has further established the Middle East as an emerging hub for cricket innovation.

Chapter Eight

Women's Cricket: The Golden Era

English Bowler Lauren Bell

"It's about showing young girls that cricket isn't just a sport—it's a platform for empowerment and achievement." —Ellyse Perry, Australian All-Rounder

We are entering a golden era for women's professional cricket. Over the past 20 years, the sport has made remarkable strides in bridging the gap between men's and women's cricket. While challenges like pay disparities and limited franchise opportunities persist, the progress is undeniable, and the outlook is brighter than ever. There has never been a better time to become a fan of women's cricket.

Many newcomers to the sport find that following women's cricket offers unique rewards and a distinct viewing experience. Women's cricket offers the chance to contribute to its growth and recognition by boosting viewership, support, and engagement. The slower bowling speeds allow for easier tracking of deliveries, and hitting boundaries and sixes feels like more significant achievements within the game's context. Female cricketers are renowned for their dedication to their craft and consistently demonstrate qualities that make them exceptional role models for fans worldwide.

Pioneering Progress

Perhaps the greatest success story in any sport is the Australian Women's National Cricket Team, widely regarded as one of the most dominant sporting teams in history. With **seven ICC Women's Cricket World Cup** titles and **six ICC Women's T20 World Cup** victories, they have set the benchmark for excellence. Their streak of **26 consecutive ODI wins from 2018 to 2021** is a testament to their consistency and professionalism. In late 2024, they demonstrated their dominance by retaining the women's Ashes, defeating England in all three T20 and ODI matches, as well as the Test match.

Key players like **Meg Lanning**, **Ellyse Perry**, and **Alyssa Healy** have been instrumental in their success, supported by a team culture rooted in skill, unity, and determination.

Globally, women's cricket is on the rise, with major tournaments like the **Women's World Cup** and the **Ashes series** drawing large audiences. **The Indian Women's Premier League (WPL)**, launched in 2023, marked a transformative milestone, providing female cricketers with a professional platform to showcase their talent. The league garnered **103 million viewers** in its inaugural season, inspiring a new generation of players to pursue cricket as a viable career.

Major franchise leagues, including the **IPL** in India, **Big Bash** in Australia, and **Vitality Blast** in England and Wales, are investing heavily in women's teams. These investments, coupled with rising attendance and viewership, reflect a growing recognition of women's cricket. For example, the **2024 Women's World Cup** in the UAE saw a **30% increase in attendance** compared to the previous tournament, with 91,000 fans attending matches.

Stephen Fry shares a story that illustrates how far cricket has come. He recounts an incident from the 1960s involving E.W. Jim Swanton, a writer for the Daily Telegraph, who burst out of the committee room at Lord's, exclaiming in a hoarse, outraged whisper, "There's a woman in there!" When it was explained to him that it was, in fact, the Queen, Jim paused to absorb this information and then replied, "Nevertheless."

From Grassroots to Professional

Cricket offers an inclusive pathway for both girls and boys. At the grassroots and junior levels, young players often train together before transitioning to separate teams around ages **13–14**. Talented girls may continue playing on boys' teams if local regulations and skill levels permit.

Women's cricket adapts to physiological differences by using a slightly smaller and lighter ball and shortening boundaries, encouraging more boundaries and sixes.

Unlike other sports that face controversies over uniforms—such as women's gymnastics and beach volleyball, where attire has sparked debates about practicality and objectification—cricket's attire for both men and women is nearly identical. This ensures that players are recognized for their athleticism and skill rather than their appearance, fostering a focus on the game itself.

Inclusivity and Cultural Shifts

The cricketing world has made significant strides toward inclusivity, both in language and practice. In **2021**, the Marylebone Cricket Club (MCC) replaced gender-specific terms like "batsman" with **"batter"** and "Man of the Match" with **"Person of the Match"** to promote gender neutrality. While some older announcers occasionally slip up and a few outdated terms with misogynistic undertones still linger, this effort to evolve language reflects a broader commitment to progress and inclusivity.

Women's cricket actively fosters inclusion for gay and bisexual players, with many openly sharing their lives on social media and some celebrated as openly married couples. The sport's inclusive policies and support networks have created a welcoming environment where players can express their true selves without fear of discrimination.

However, the inclusion of trans women athletes remains a complex and evolving issue, with varying restricting regulations across different cricket boards and governing bodies. Discussions about ensuring fairness and inclusivity continue, but the path to full inclusion is still being navigated.

Challenges and Future Goals

Despite its successes, women's cricket still faces challenges. The number of women's teams in major franchises remains lower than men's, and a significant **salary gap** persists. To sustain growth, it's crucial to continue investing in grassroots programs, competitive opportunities, and professional leagues, particularly in non-traditional cricketing nations like the U.S.

To achieve parity, expanding broadcast coverage for women's cricket is essential. While platforms like Willow have done a commendable job, the sport needs to be featured on a wider range of channels and in more accessible spaces to reach new audiences. A focused effort on **social media platforms** is equally critical, harnessing the power of digital engagement to showcase matches, highlight players, and build a dedicated community of supporters. Women's cricket has already produced iconic superstars in countries like Australia, England, and India; however, for the sport to thrive in the U.S., it is vital to cultivate and celebrate homegrown female cricketing legends. Acknowledging and promoting these athletes will help expand the sport's reach and inspire the next generation of players and fans.

The U.S. Women's National Cricket Team

The U.S. Women's National Cricket Team represents the United States on the international stage and is governed by **USA Cricket**, an Associate Member of the **International Cricket Council (ICC)** since 1965. As a developing force in global women's cricket, the team has shown increasing potential, particularly within the **ICC Americas region**.

The team made its international debut in **2009** at the Americas Women's Championship in Fort Lauderdale and earned **T20 International (T20I) status** in 2018. This milestone allowed them to compete in official ICC T20I matches. Although they have yet to qualify for major tournaments like the **ICC Women's T20 World Cup**, they have demonstrated consistent progress in global qualifiers

In an exciting development, the team recently won the **ICC Women's T20 World Cup Americas Qualifier** in Buenos Aires. Competing in a double round-robin tournament against Canada, Brazil, and Argentina, the U.S. team emerged victorious, securing a spot in the **Global Qualifier**, a ten-team tournament where the top teams will advance to the **2026 ICC Women's T20 World Cup** in England and Wales.

Key players such as **Sindhu Sriharsha**, **Geetika Kodali**, and **Tara Norris** have been instrumental in the team's performance. Leadership is currently provided by **Anika Kolan**, supported by head coach **Hilton Moreeng**.

USA Cricket is also committed to fostering the growth of cricket among women and youth, focusing on **grassroots programs** and expanding **competitive opportunities** to strengthen the team. Despite challenges such as limited infrastructure and competition from more established sports, the team's active participation in regional tournaments highlights their resilience and determination.

The U.S. Women's National Cricket Team symbolizes the rising popularity of cricket in the United States and represents the sport's potential to flourish in non-traditional cricketing nations.

The Afghanistan Women's Team in Exile

Not all parts of the world fully embrace progress in women's sports, and the plight of the Afghanistan women's cricket team underscores the challenges that persist. Since the Taliban's return to power in **2021**, women's sports have been effectively banned, leaving female cricketers in Afghanistan facing threats, intimidation, and a complete halt in the development of the sport. This has sparked global outrage and calls for the **International Cricket Council (ICC)** to take action.

As a requirement for Full Membership, the ICC mandates that nations maintain both men's and women's national teams. Despite Afghanistan's failure to meet this criterion, it has retained Full Member status. This inconsistency has drawn significant criticism, with human rights advocates, politicians, and cricket fans worldwide calling for boycotts and further scrutiny.

A Dangerous Escape

In response to this dire situation, a group of dedicated volunteers, including former Australian cricketer Mel Jones and Emma Staples, stepped in to help. They secured **emergency humanitarian visas** from the Australian government for the exiled female cricketers, granting them a chance at safety.

In a perilous and heart-wrenching journey, **22 players and their families** left Afghanistan. To pass through Taliban checkpoints, they had to provide cover stories such as attending a family wedding or seeking urgent medical care. Once in Australia, the players settled in **Canberra** and **Melbourne**, where they continued their cricket careers by joining local club teams.

In January 2025, a significant milestone was reached with the formation of the **Afghan Women's XI** in exile. This team, made up of players who had previously represented Afghanistan's national team, played their inaugural match against a **Cricket Without Borders XI** at Junction Oval in Melbourne.

A Symbol of Resilience

The creation of the Afghan Women's XI represents much more than cricket—it is a **beacon of resilience and defiance** against oppression. For millions of Afghan women denied basic rights, this team symbolizes hope and resistance to gender discrimination.

Both **Cricket Australia** and the Australian government have been instrumental in supporting these women, providing resources to rebuild their lives and promoting inclusivity in the sport. The Afghan Women's XI stands as a powerful reminder that even under the most challenging circumstances, cricket can serve as a platform for empowerment and unity.

Chapter Nine

Major Cricket Leagues Around The World

Team rivalries, stylish uniforms, a competative regular season, and playoffs are hallmarks of modern sports entertainment. Behind the scenes, the business side of sports—encompassing multi-million-dollar salaries, TV and streaming rights, stadium deals, merchandise, endorsements, and billion-dollar franchises—plays a pivotal role in sustaining and growing these leagues. While this business aspect is often overshadowed by the thrill of the game, it is the driving force behind the accessibility and global appeal of all major sports.

Franchise leagues represent both the present and future of cricket. In 1989, Jerry Jones purchased the Dallas Cowboys for $140 million; today, the franchise is estimated to be worth $10 billion. Similarly, the Indian Premier League (IPL) features top teams valued at over $120 million, with predictions suggesting that some franchises could reach $1 billion in the coming decades. Despite being only 17 years old, the IPL already boasts a total valuation exceeding $15 billion.

These leagues attract significant investment, drawing in celebrity owners such as Bollywood superstars. This influx of funding, coupled with widespread fan support, has led to numerous positive developments. Players now enjoy lucrative contracts, and the establishment of leagues like the Women's Premier League (WPL) has enabled many women cricketers to pursue the sport professionally, gaining access to world-class training and facilities.

In the United States, cricket is steadily gaining traction at both major and minor league levels. Major League Cricket (MLC) offers an exciting opportunity for fans to witness the sport's growth firsthand—akin to experiencing the early Super Bowls or World Series. As new teams and stadiums emerge across the country, cricket is poised to establish itself as a prominent feature of the American sports landscape. By supporting these leagues, fans can play a crucial role in helping U.S. cricket develop into a competitive force on the global stage.

U.S. Major League Cricket (MLC)

Major League Cricket (MLC) represents a pivotal chapter in the development of cricket in the United States, combining top-tier talent, strategic investments, and world-class facilities to captivate fans nationwide. While MLC may not yet rival the Indian Premier League (IPL) in terms of fan base, it offers something unique: the excitement of experiencing matches live, with games conveniently scheduled across U.S. time zones.

Launched in 2023 with the backing of influential investors and strategic partnerships, MLC has swiftly established a foundation for success. Notably, Microsoft plays a crucial role as a key investor, with CEO Satya Nadella committed to integrating cutting-edge technology into the league's infrastructure. This funding attracts top coaching and support staff from around the globe, enabling MLC to mirror the IPL's winning formula.

MLC games utilize the popular T20 format, beginning with round-robin group stages before advancing to knockout rounds and culminating in a championship final. Fans worldwide follow the action through extensive broadcast and streaming rights, including Willow.tv, the premier U.S. platform for cricket.

Each season, player drafts and auctions ensure competitive balance and distribution of international and domestic talent. Teams may sign players to single-year or multi-year contracts, with a maximum of nine overseas players per team and six allowed in the starting lineup for each match. To foster the development of domestic cricket, each roster must include at least one under-23 U.S. player and nine local players from America. This structure guarantees the inclusion of promising American talent while maintaining global standards.

The U.S. national teams stand to benefit significantly from MLC, as the league serves as an elite development platform. By combining international and domestic expertise, MLC not only elevates the quality of U.S. cricket but also showcases its players' potential to other leagues worldwide. Additionally, MLC invests in promoting cricket at schools, colleges, and youth levels through camps, coaching clinics, and tournaments, creating a robust grassroots pipeline.

Though MLC is still in its infancy, its commitment to growth is evident in its inaugural setup. The six founding franchises represent key regions in the U.S., with plans to expand into additional cities and eventually establish a women's league. So far, matches have been hosted at the Grand Prairie Cricket Stadium in Dallas and Church Street Park in Morrisville, NC—strategic locations chosen to capitalize on quality facilities and minimize travel.

Team	Ownership/Identity	Stadium Plans
Los Angeles Knight Riders	Owned by Knight Riders Group, which also owns the IPL's Kolkata Knight Riders.	No stadium has been announced.
San Francisco Unicorns	The name reflects the tech sector and the identity of Silicon Valley.	No stadium has been announced.
Texas Super Kings	Part of the Super Kings Group, which also operates IPL's Chennai Super Kings.	Home matches will be played at Prairie View Cricket Complex in Grand Prairie, TX.
MI New York	Owned by Indiawin Sports, which also owns IPL's Mumbai Indians.	Plans to host matches at Marine Park Stadium in Brooklyn (10,000 capacity).
Seattle Orcas	The name emphasizes the Pacific Northwest identity.	Plans to play at Lumen Field in downtown Seattle (40,000 capacity).
Washington Freedom	Owned by Indian-born entrepreneur Sanjay Govil; the team won the 2024 championship.	Actively seeking a home stadium.

You can show your support for Major League Cricket by purchasing merchandise for your favorite team at the official MLC store (shop.majorleaguecricket.com) or during games. Wearing the replica jersey of your favorite player, is a great way to celebrate your fandom and bring visibility to the league. By actively engaging with MLC—whether through attending matches, watching broadcasts, or sharing the excitement online—you contribute to the growth of cricket in the U.S., paving the way for its success on the global stage.

U.S. Minor League Cricket (MiLC)

Minor League Cricket (MiLC) is a semi-professional T20 league in the U.S. that serves as a feeder system for Major League Cricket (MLC) while also expanding the cricket fan base in the country. The league features high-level international players, but each team must include a minimum of seven U.S. players, emphasizing the development of local talent through youth academies and training programs.

The league consists of **26 teams** divided into **four** divisions: Eastern, Southern, Western, and Central. Games are held during the summer, with the top teams from each division advancing to the playoffs and ultimately competing in the finals.

Although MiLC is still in its early stages, the league has made professional cricket more accessible to fans across the U.S. Venues are being finalized, so fans are encouraged to check the MiLC website (www.minorleaguecricket.com) for the latest updates. Matches are also live-streamed on YouTube, allowing fans to enjoy games from anywhere while benefiting from insightful commentary that helps demystify the game's nuances.

Eastern Division

Manhattan Yorkers
New England Eagles
New Jersey Somerset Cavaliers
New Jersey Stallions
Empire State Titans
The Philadelphians

Southern Division

Atlanta Lightning
Baltimore Royals (formerly
DC Hawks)
Ft. Lauderdale Lions
Morrisville Raptors
(Morrisville NC)
Orlando Galaxy
Atlanta Fire

Western Division

East Bay Blazers
Golden State Grizzlies
Los Angeles Lashings
San Diego Surf Riders
Seattle Thunderbolts
Silicon Valley Strikers

Central Division

Chicago Kingsmen
Chicago Tigers
Dallas Xforia Giants
Dallas Mustangs
Houston Hurricanes
Lone Star Athletics
Michigan Cricket Stars
St. Louis Americans

MiLC offers a unique and intimate cricket experience for fans. Matches allow for close interaction with players, fostering a family-friendly atmosphere where autographs and casual conversations are commonplace. Additionally, the league's commitment to nurturing young talent will undoubtedly shape the future of U.S. cricket, enhancing its competitiveness on the global stage.

By attending MiLC games or streaming them online, fans not only enjoy high-quality cricket but also support the grassroots efforts necessary to grow the sport across the country.

Indian Premier League (IPL)

The Indian Premier League (IPL) is by far the largest and most lucrative cricket league in the world, evolving from a startup concept in 2008 into a truly international spectacle, broadcast in 120 countries. Often referred to as the "festival of cricket" in India, the

IPL merges high-energy games, global viewership, and cultural flair to create an unparalleled sporting event.

Unparalleled Global Reach

The scale of the IPL's growth is remarkable. To provide perspective, the National Football League (NFL) attracts 200 million unique viewers in the U.S. per season, with 186 million watching the Super Bowl® worldwide. In contrast, the IPL commands an estimated **500 million unique viewers per season in India alone.** In 2023, the IPL Final drew a staggering 505 million viewers on the Star Sports Network, highlighting its immense popularity.

Tournament Format and Structure

Lasting approximately two months between March and May, the IPL features **60 to 74 matches** each season. Currently composed of **10 franchises**, the league is expected to expand further in the coming years. Matches are held across various cities in India, with teams competing in a **round-robin series**, ensuring that each team faces every other team at least once.

The playoffs consist of:

1. **Qualifier 1**: The top two ranked teams compete for a direct berth in the finals.
2. **Eliminator**: The third and fourth place teams face off, with the winner advancing.
3. **Qualifier 2**: The loser of Qualifier 1 plays the winner of the Eliminator, determining the final spot in the championship game.

This format provides a second chance for the top-seeded teams, adding strategic depth to the playoffs.

Revolutionizing Cricket Through Technology

The IPL has set a benchmark for the use of **innovative technology** in cricket. From advanced analytics and real-time player tracking systems to immersive viewing experiences, the league ensures fans stay connected to every moment of the game.

Record-Breaking Stadiums and Attendance

India's cricket venues are as grand as its enthusiasm for the game. The **Narendra Modi Stadium** in Ahmedabad, with a capacity of **132,000** fans, exemplifies this scale. Average match attendance ranges between **30,000 and 60,000**, depending on the venue, while ticket prices remain accessible, starting at $5 USD. Premium options, including luxury seating and VIP packages, cater to those seeking a more exclusive experience.

Entertainment and Player Celebrity

The IPL is known for blending cricket with entertainment. Fans can enjoy cheerleaders, live music, themed events, and celebrity performances during matches. Player salaries reflect the league's financial power, with top athletes like Virat Kohli earning $1.8 million USD per season, along with $30 million in endorsements. The IPL's lucrative contracts and global exposure have transformed players into household names and idols for millions.

Inspiring T20 Leagues Worldwide

The success of the IPL has inspired the creation of other prominent T20 leagues, including the **Australian Big Bash League** and the **Caribbean Premier League (CPL)**. For fans in the U.S. and Canada, IPL matches are accessible via the Willow app, making it easier than ever to join the worldwide celebration of cricket.

Women's Indian Premier League (WIPL)

The Women's Indian Premier League (WIPL), launched in 2023, is modeled after the IPL but features several distinct characteristics. Established to harness the growing popularity of women's cricket in India, the league provides aspiring players with the platform and resources necessary to achieve professional and national-level success.

The WIPL began with **five teams** during its inaugural season and is poised for expansion, with plans to add more franchises and extend the season's duration. As viewership continues to grow both in India and internationally, the league has elevated the global profile of women's cricket, ensuring greater visibility and recognition for female athletes.

Format and Venue

Unlike the traditional home-and-away format of the IPL, WIPL matches are played at select venues, resulting in a condensed season lasting **three** weeks. Among the teams, only the **Mumbai Indians** and **Delhi Capitals** share names with their IPL counterparts; the remaining teams boast unique identities that distinguish them from their male equivalents.

Player Auction and Salaries

The inaugural player auction in 2023 featured top international cricketers from India, Australia, England, and New Zealand, alongside rising domestic talent. To maintain a balance of national representation, league regulations limited the number of foreign players.

While player salaries remain modest compared to the IPL, the highest-paid athlete earns **$120,000 USD** for the three-week season—a respectable amount that reflects the league's growing financial strength. The WIPL has already had a transformative impact on the sport, offering financial support, advanced facilities, and structured player development initiatives. Many players who excel in the WIPL are likely to secure spots on their national teams.

Inspiring the Next Generation

The WIPL's emphasis on showcasing professional female cricketers as role models has sparked interest among young girls, boosting grassroots participation in the sport. By providing accessible opportunities and inspiring stories, the league is helping to build a sustainable future for women's cricket in India and beyond.

Where to Watch

Fans in the **U.S. and Canada** can tune into WIPL matches on Willow, with the season typically aligning with the IPL in March. The league's success and accessibility ensure that cricket enthusiasts everywhere can celebrate and support the rise of women's cricket.

Big Bash League (BBL)

Launched by Cricket Australia in 2011 after the success of the IPL, the men's T20 Big Bash League (BBL) has grown into one of the world's premier T20 competitions. The league features **eight** teams, some of which share identities with their female counterparts, while others have distinct branding.

Season Structure and Playoffs

The BBL's **61-game season** runs during the **Australian** summer, from December to February. Teams compete in a **round-robin** series, with each team facing all others at least once.

The playoff structure includes:

1. **Qualifier**: The top two ranked teams face off, with the winner advancing directly to the final.
2. **Eliminator**: The third and fourth place teams compete, with the winner progressing.
3. **Knockout**: The Eliminator winner faces the loser of the Qualifier for the final spot in the championship.

This system provides the highest-seeded teams with an additional opportunity to reach the final, ensuring a balance between competitiveness and fairness.

Logistical Challenges and Geographic Scale

The league's venues span the vast distances of Australia, presenting unique logistical challenges. For instance, **Perth Stadium** in Western Australia and **Blundstone Arena** in Tasmania are separated by **1,864**miles. Despite this, the league successfully delivers high-quality cricket to fans across the country.

Entertainment and Atmosphere

True to the Australian spirit, the BBL emphasizes creating a **family-friendly, festive atmosphere.** Games feature **colorful uniforms, music, fireworks,** cheerleaders, and other entertainment elements designed to captivate fans of all ages. This approach has made the league a staple of the Australian summer.

Player Salaries and Talent Pool

Operating under a **salary cap of $1.2** million USD, the BBL offers top salaries of approximately **$165,000** USD, which can increase with match fees, sponsorships, and incentives. While the league primarily showcases Australian talent, many top **international cricketers** also participate, enhancing its global appeal.

As a breeding ground for Australian cricket, the BBL provides young players with invaluable exposure to international competition, helping to shape the next generation of Australian stars.

Women's Big Bash League (WBBL)

Established in 2015, Australia's Women's Big Bash League (WBBL) has quickly emerged as one of the premier T20 competitions for female cricket talent. Featuring **eight** teams, the league showcases elite players while enhancing the growth and visibility of women's cricket.

Season Structure and Playoffs

The WBBL runs from **October to December** and lasts **4 to 6** weeks, making it slightly shorter than its male counterpart. Each team competes in **14 regular-season** matches, followed by a playoff series and final, mirroring the format of the men's Big Bash League (BBL).

Player Salaries and Growth

Operating under a **salary cap of $464,000** USD, the WBBL offers top salaries of **$85,000** USD, supplemented by match fees, sponsorship deals, and performance incentives. A five-year agreement guarantees steady annual salary increases, making female cricketers in Australia the **highest-paid women's athletes** in Australian team sports.

Impact and Community Initiatives

The WBBL has had a transformative effect on women's cricket in Australia, inspiring young girls to take up the sport and providing a platform for athletes to excel. The league supports grassroots initiatives through **cricket clinics** and **development** programs, promoting participation and nurturing talent at all levels.

Vitality Blast/T20 Blast

The men's **Vitality Blast**, launched in 2003 under the name Twenty20 Cup, is the first official T20 cricket league. It has played a pivotal role in popularizing the T20 format, paving the way for the establishment of numerous T20 leagues worldwide. While the players embody energy and dynamism, the league's name originates from its primary sponsor, the Vitality Health and Insurance Company.

Season and Structure

Matches are held across **England and Wales** over a **6- to 8-week period** during the English summer, officially spanning from **May to September**. The league's schedule is carefully aligned with the English domestic and international cricket calendar, avoiding conflicts with major events.

The men's league consists of **18 teams**, divided into the **North Group** and the **South Group**. Each team plays **14 group-stage matches**, facing some opponents twice and others only once.

After the group stage, the top 8 teams—4 from each group—advance to the **quarter-finals**, followed by the highly anticipated **Finals Day**. This event, held at **Edgbaston Cricket Ground in Birmingham**, features two semi-final matches and a final on the same day, making it a marquee highlight of the English cricket calendar.

Player Recruitment and Salaries

Each team is allowed to sign up to **two overseas players**, competing to attract high-profile international talent. Unlike the IPL, there is no **player auction or draft**; teams negotiate directly with players.

- **Top Salaries**: Up to **$160,000 USD per season**
- **Average Salaries**: Between **$24,000 and $61,000 USD**
- **Emerging Player Salaries**: Between **$12,000 and $24,000 USD**

While compensation is significantly lower than in the IPL, it is comparable to salaries offered in the BBL. The Vitality Blast provides young English players from cricket academies and lower leagues with the opportunity to showcase their talent, ultimately aiming for progression to other leagues or national team selection.

Women's Vitality Blast/T20 Blast

An exciting transformation awaits women's English cricket in **2025** as the Vitality Blast introduces a **fully aligned women's league**, marking a significant milestone for gender equality in the sport. This development coincides with the discontinuation of the Charlotte Edwards Cup, paving the way for a new era of professionalism and visibility in women's domestic cricket.

New Professional Structure

The England and Wales Cricket Board (ECB) will launch **eight new professional women's teams**, primarily competing under their county names. This initiative aims to significantly elevate the standards of women's cricket across England and Wales, backed by substantial investment from the ECB.

As announced by the ECB: *"The new professional structure will see £8 million of new funding per year invested in women's domestic cricket by 2027, bringing annual investment in this area to £19 million. This initiative could lead to an **80% increase** in the number of professional female players in England and Wales by 2029."*

This commitment, approximately **$10.4 million USD** per year in new funding, will drive annual investment to **$24.7 million USD** by 2027, ensuring the growth and sustainability of women's cricket.

Integrated Match Schedule

The 2025 schedule will feature **doubleheaders**, with a women's match played in the morning followed by the corresponding men's match in the afternoon. Typically, the men's and women's matches involve the same teams; for instance, if the **London Spirit** competes against the **Manchester Originals** in the women's game, the men's teams of **London Spirit** and **Manchester Originals** will also face off later in the day. This groundbreaking format marks a significant step toward achieving equality in the sport. By synchronizing schedules for both leagues, the ECB underscores its commitment to elevating women's cricket alongside the men's league, providing fans with an inclusive and engaging experience.

Caribbean Premier League (CPL)

The **Caribbean Premier League (CPL)** is renowned as one of the most popular T20 leagues globally. Its vibrant atmosphere distinguishes it from other competitions, showcasing the unique personalities of each Caribbean island through **colorful attire, music, and festive elements.** Matches are played in time zones that aligns well with U.S. audiences and are broadcast live on **Willow**, making them easily accessible to CPL fans worldwide.

Platform for Talent

The CPL serves as a vital platform for local Caribbean talent to compete alongside some of the most renowned international cricket stars. Teams can sign up to **four international players**, many of whom are acquired through a **player draft** or direct contracts. Beyond the competitive appeal, players enjoy the opportunity to immerse themselves in the **Caribbean's lively culture** during August and September.

The region has produced some of the finest cricketers in the world. Representing a unifying spirit, the **West Indies teams** bring together cricket-playing Caribbean islands into a **single national team**, boasting an impressive track record in international competitions.

The current teams are:

- Barbados Royals (formerly Barbados Tridents)
- Guyana Amazon Warriors
- Jamaica Tallawahs
- St. Kitts & Nevis Patriots
- Saint Lucia Kings (formerly St. Lucia Zouks)
- Trinbago Knight Riders (affiliated with the IPL's Kolkata Knight Riders)

League Structure

The CPL employs a **round-robin format**, with teams competing against one another in the group stage.

The playoffs consist of:

1. **Qualifier**: The top two teams face off, with the winner advancing directly to the final.

2. **Eliminator**: The third and fourth place teams compete, with the winner moving on.

3. **Knockout**: The Eliminator winner plays the Qualifier loser for the final spot in the championship.

This structure allows the **Qualifier loser** a second chance to reach the final, fostering competitiveness and excitement in the playoffs.

Cultural Impact and Development

The CPL has significantly contributed to the development of **Caribbean cricket talent**, offering young players opportunities to showcase their skills on an international stage. The league has revitalized interest in cricket across the islands, drawing large crowds and engaging fans of all ages. Its celebration of Caribbean culture and its role in globalizing the sport make the CPL a truly unique and impactful competition.

The Hundred: A Unique Annual Tournament

The **Hundred** is a distinctive annual tournament held in England and Wales, featuring a format that reflects its name. Introduced to bring a fresh dynamic to the sport, The Hundred combines innovative gameplay with an inclusive structure, making it a standout event on the cricketing calendar.

The tournament typically takes place in **late July or early August**, accommodating players involved in other tournaments and international series. Matches are hosted at multiple cricket grounds, creating a festival-like atmosphere throughout the region.

Teams and Inclusivity

The competition features **eight franchise** teams, including notable names such as the **Southern Brave** and **Welsh** Fire. A unique hallmark of The Hundred is its integration of **men's and women's** teams, which share **uniforms,** schedules, and fanbases. For example, a day of cricket might include the **women's London Spirit** facing off against the **Trent Rockets** in the morning, followed by the men's

Spirit and Rockets teams in the afternoon, creating a fully immersive experience for fans.

Player Selection and Salaries

Players are recruited through a **draft system**, inviting both international superstars and domestic players to participate.

- **Men's salaries:** Range from **$39K to $252K USD**.
- **Women's salaries:** Range from **$13K to $39K USD**, with expectations for gradual increases as the league grows.

Many national team players participate, making The Hundred a prime opportunity to witness some of the sport's greatest talents in action.

Tournament Format

The group stage involves **four home and four away matches** in a **round-robin format**. Points are awarded as follows:

- **2 points** for a win.
- **1 point** for a No Result.

The standings are determined by points, with **Net Run Rate (NRR)** serving as a tiebreaker.

- The **first-place team** advances directly to the Final.
- The **second- and third-place teams** compete in a playoff, with the winner progressing to the Final.

The Final is traditionally held at **Lord's Cricket Ground**, revered as the **Home of Cricket**.

A Celebration of Equality and Entertainment

The Hundred is one of the most enjoyable tournaments, celebrated for lessening the emphasis on national pride and creating a relaxed, inclusive environment. The synchronized play schedules for men's and women's teams highlight cricket's commitment to equality, with teams actively supporting one another on and off the field. This collaborative spirit, combined with thrilling gameplay, makes The Hundred an event worth celebrating each year.

Chapter Ten

Global Tournaments and Iconic Clashes

The 2028 Olympics: Cricket's Return to the Games

Cricket is set to return to the **Olympics** in **Los Angeles in 2028** after a 128-year absence! The last time cricket appeared in the Olympics was at the **1900 Paris** Games, with only **Great Britain** and **France** competing. This monumental reintroduction presents an incredible opportunity to showcase cricket to an American audience.

Both men's and women's cricket teams will compete in the 2028 Olympics, participating in **T20 tournaments** featuring **six teams** each. As the host nation, the **United States** is guaranteed a spot in both competitions. This historic inclusion not only introduces the sport to a broader American audience but also has the potential to ignite greater interest and integrate cricket into the fabric of mainstream American sports culture.

ICC Men's T20 World Cup

A Historic Upset by the U.S. in 2024

The 2024 Men's T20 World Cup, co-hosted by the **United States** and the **West Indies**, brought cricket to the forefront in the U.S. with a historic upset. The **U.S. men's team** shocked the cricketing world by defeating **Pakistan**, one of the strongest teams, in a thrilling **overtime Super Over** victory.

- **Pakistan's First Innings**: 159 runs, 7 wickets lost.
- **U.S. Heroics**: Jaskaran Malhotra's last-ball boundary tied the match at 159.
- **Super Over**: The U.S. scored **18 runs**, while Pakistan managed only **13**, thanks to exceptional bowling by **Ali Khan**.

Although the U.S. was eliminated in the **Super 8** stage, their victory against Pakistan secured **automatic qualification** for the next World Cup and demonstrated the team's growing potential on the world stage.

Tournament Format

The **T20 World Cup** began in **2007** and is held **every two years**, barring scheduling disruptions. Teams qualify through a combination of ICC rankings and regional tournaments. Key stages include:

- **Super 12 Stage**: Twelve teams, divided into two groups of six, play in a round-robin format.
- **Knockout Stage**: The top two teams from each group advance to the semi-finals and, subsequently, the final.

The next Men's T20 World Cup will be co-hosted by **India** and **Sri Lanka** in **February 2026**, promising another thrilling chapter in international cricket.

ICC Women's T20 World Cup

The **2026 Women's T20 World Cup** will be co-hosted by **England and Wales** in **June 2026**, featuring **12 teams**, an increase from 10 in 2024. The tournament will follow a qualification structure similar to the men's competition, with the host nation automatically qualifying.

Matches are expected to take place at iconic venues such as **Lord's Cricket Ground** and **The Oval**, making travel convenient for fans thanks to England's excellent train network. Australia continues to be the dominant force in women's T20 cricket, holding six titles, but underdog stories like **New Zealand's 2024 victory over South Africa** highlight the growing competitiveness of the game.

In an exciting development, the U.S. Women's National Cricket Team recently won the **ICC Women's T20 World Cup Americas Qualifier** in Buenos Aires. Competing in a double round-robin tournament against Canada, Brazil, and Argentina, the U.S. team emerged victorious, securing a spot in the **Global Qualifier**, a ten-team tournament where the top teams will advance to the **2026 ICC Women's T20 World Cup** in England and Wales.

ICC Cricket World Cup (ODI)

Upcoming Events

- **2025 Women's ODI World Cup**: Hosted by **India** in **September–October 2025**.

- **2027 Men's ODI World Cup**: Co-hosted by **South Africa**, **Zimbabwe**, and **Namibia** in **October–November 2027**.

- **2031 Men's ODI World Cup**: Co-hosted by **India** and **Bangladesh**.

Qualification Process

The **ODI World Cup** is held every **four years**, featuring the world's best teams. The teams that qualify are determined through:

1. **ICC Super League**: The top **eight teams**, including the host nation, qualify directly based on points earned during eight bilateral series.

2. **World Cup Qualifiers**: Additional teams compete for the final two spots through a group stage and knockout rounds.

3. **Associate Member Leagues**: Teams from lower-ranked nations, such as those in the ICC Cricket World Cup League 2, also have a pathway to qualification.

Ultimately, **ten teams** compete in a **round-robin group stage**, with the top teams advancing to the semi-finals and then the final.

U.S. Women's Team

The U.S. women's cricket team earned **ODI status in 2022** and continues to compete internationally. Their progress, including tours such as their **5-match ODI series in Zimbabwe**, showcases the growing potential of U.S. women's cricket in the 50-over format.

ICC World Test Championship: The Ultimate Prize

The **ICC World Test Championship**, held every **two years**, recognizes the best team in traditional cricket. Points are earned through bilateral Test series, with rankings determined by the percentage of points earned. The top **two teams** then compete in a one-off Test at a **neutral venue** to crown the champion.

- **2021 Champion: New Zealand**

- **2023 Champion: Australia**

- **Future Finals**: England will host the next three Championships in **2027**, **2029**, and **2031**.

Currently, there is **no women's Test Championship**, but efforts to promote the format may expand its scope in the future.

The Ashes: England vs Australia's Historic Rivalry

Few sporting events rival the **Ashes** in terms of history and intensity. This legendary Test series between **England** and **Australia** began in **1882** after England suffered a home defeat at The Oval. The series derives its name from a satirical obituary of English cricket published in a British newspaper: *"The body will be cremated, and the ashes taken to Australia."*

Key Features

- Held **every two years**, alternating between England and Australia.

- Consists of **five Test matches**, each lasting up to five days.

- Symbolized by the **Ashes urn**, displayed at the **Marylebone Cricket Club** (MCC) in London.

The Ashes represents more than just cricket; it embodies **national pride** and fierce rivalry. Players who excel become legends in their countries, inspiring future generations. For fans looking to delve deeper, **Stephen Fry's podcast**, *Legends of the Ashes*, offers a comprehensive exploration of the series' rich history.

Chapter Eleven
Discover Cricket Resources

Willow TV: Your Cricket Channel

In the U.S., **Willow TV®** offers the best value for cricket fans. As of this writing, a subscription costs **$9.99 per month** or **$79.99 per year**, with occasional introductory specials. Willow provides access to major matches worldwide, including the **IPL**, **Vitality Blast**, **MLC**, **World Cup**, and **international series**. Its coverage of **women's cricket** is particularly impressive.

Willow allows you to watch matches in two ways:

1. **Real-time Viewing**: Watch live matches as they air, but note that pause and rewind functionality is unavailable. Be prepared to adjust to time zone differences, which may require late nights or early mornings in the U.S.

2. **Full Match Replays**: After each innings or every few hours during longer formats, Willow posts replays that allow you to fast-forward, rewind, and resume watching later. Matches remain accessible for at least a week.

Willow TV is compatible with web browsers, iOS®, Android®, Apple TV®, Roku, Amazon Fire TV®, Xbox One®, Android TV®, and Chromecast®. It may also be available through **Dish®**, **Spectrum®**, **Optimum®**, or **FIOS®** channel subscriptions. Visit www.willow.tv/subscribe.

ESPNcricinfo

For cricket news, schedules, and live updates, **ESPN Cricinfo** remains the go-to resource. Free to use across web and iOS/Android apps, it provides a seamless user interface filled with everything a cricket enthusiast could want.

Features

- **Live Match Updates**: Follow scores, detailed match information, live commentary, and player stats.

- **Match Commentary**: Gain clarity on complex plays or match events through running commentary.

- **Series Overview**: View current and upcoming tours, leagues, and matches under the "Series" section. Add events to your calendar, with times displayed in your local time zone.

- **News and Photos**: Access top stories, live coverage, and stunning cricket photography.

Whether you're tracking your favorite player or seeking updates during weather delays, ESPN Cricinfo ensures you stay informed. Visit www.espncricinfo.com for more information.

Cricbuzz

Similar to ESPN Cricinfo, **Cricbuzz** offers cricket news, schedules, and updates via its website and free apps. Its partnership with Willow integrates live content directly into the Cricbuzz platform, making it another top choice for cricket fans. Visit www.cricbuzz.com for details.

ICC: International Cricket Council

The **International Cricket Council (ICC)** governs global cricket, overseeing the ICC Code of Conduct, match regulations, and the Decision Review System. The ICC also selects match officials for international games and operates an **Anti-Corruption Unit**.

Key Resources

- **Events**: Information on all ICC-sanctioned tournaments.

- **Live Broadcasts**: Selected events are available on the ICC web site.

- **Rankings**: Player and team rankings across all formats.

- **Rules**: Comprehensive explanations of cricket laws and regulations.

- **Tickets and Streaming**: Free streaming of select matches not available on Willow, along with tickets to major events.

The ICC website offers valuable resources for learning about cricket's intricacies while staying updated on upcoming fixtures. Visit www.icc-cricket.com for more information.

USA Cricket

USA Cricket manages the U.S. men's and women's national teams, aiming for full ICC membership by **2030**. The organization also oversees **Under-19 teams**, ensuring future talent development through events like the **U19 World Cup**.

Visit USA Cricket's website for schedules, team updates, and initiatives to grow cricket in America. Visit www.usacricket.org for more information.

U.S. Major and Minor Cricket Leagues

The official websites for **MLC** and **MiLC** provide league schedules, ticket information, merchandise, and team details. While visually appealing, these sites could benefit from improved functionality and more frequent updates.

Social media accounts offer additional insights:

- **YouTube**: www.youtube.com/@MLC_Network | www.youtube.com/c/MinorLeagueCricket

- **Instagram**: www.instagram.com/mlcricketusa | www.instagram.com/milcusa

- **Facebook**: www.facebook.com/MLC | www.facebook.com/MiLCUSA

Visit www.majorleaguecricket.com and www.minorleaguecricket.com for more information.

Cricket Council of the United States of America (CCUSA)

CCUSA focuses on promoting cricket at all levels in the U.S., from grassroots initiatives to professional franchises. The organization hosts major competitions in Florida, including:

- **President's Cup**
- **Legends Cup**
- **USA T10**
- **U.S. Open**

CCUSA's efforts aim to grow cricket's footprint nationwide while engaging sponsors, advertisers, and investors. Visit www.ccusa.info for more information.

YouTube

YouTube offers a treasure trove of cricket content. The **MLC Network** and **Minor League Cricket** channels live-stream matches, including MiLC games, making it easy to follow teams from anywhere.

Commentators **Nick Hayes** and **Aaman Patel** are particularly knowledgeable, offering insights into American players and their roles in world cricket. Both also contribute to the **Emerging Cricket Podcast**. Visit www.youtube.com/@MLC_Network and www.youtube.com/c/MinorLeagueCricket for more information.

The Emerging Cricket Podcast

Highlighting cricket's growth in emerging nations, the **Emerging Cricket Podcast** explores stories from Associate Members striving for recognition. The network includes a U.S.-focused show called **Big Innings**, hosted by Nick Hayes and Aaman Patel. Visit https://podcast.emergingcricket.com/ for more information.

The Laws of Cricket

Codified in **1787** by the **Marylebone Cricket Club (MCC)**, the **Laws of Cricket** remain the definitive guide to the game. While the rules have evolved over time, their foundation stems from an early meeting held at a London pub.

Benjamin Franklin famously brought a copy of these laws to the U.S., helping introduce the sport. Today, they're available online for those interested in cricket's technical framework. Visit https://www.lords.org/mcc/the-laws-of-cricket for more information.

Chapter Twelve

Understanding Cricket Equipment

If you decide to take up cricket, be prepared for a **significant investment** in gear. While fielding and bowling require minimal equipment, protective gear is essential for batting and wicketkeeping. Cricket clubs may offer basic equipment sets, but higher-quality items will need to be purchased individually.

If you're looking for a sport with minimal gear, perhaps **sumo wrestling** is a better choice!

The Cricket Ball

Stock up on **cricket balls**—you'll need them! Cricket balls come in various colors for different formats:

- **White**: Standard for ODI and T20 matches, ideal for night games.
- **Red**: Used in Test matches, best for visibility in daylight.

- **Pink**: Used in day-night Test matches, offering a compromise for visibility under natural and artificial lighting.

Women's cricket balls are **slightly smaller and lighter**, ensuring fairness and competitiveness. If you're curious, you can purchase a couple of balls in different colors for practice or display.

Essential Batting Gear

Cricket Bat

Your bat will be your closest companion—choose wisely!

- **Materials**: More affordable bats use **Kashmir Willow**, while premium bats are crafted from **English Willow**.
- **Grains**: Higher-quality bats have **straight grain patterns**; more grains generally indicate better performance.

- **Customization**: Handles come in **round** or **oval shapes** and vary in **length** (short, normal, long). Bats also differ in weight, so pick one suited to your comfort and batting style.

Maintenance:

- **Oil your bat** before its first use and annually. Use **anti-scuff sheets** to maintain its appearance and delay re-oiling needs.

- **Knock In**: Like breaking in a baseball glove, knocking in your bat hardens it to prevent cracking. Use a mallet or old ball, gently tapping the surface for **10–15 minutes daily for 2–3 weeks**. Proper care ensures your bat can last a lifetime.

Batting Helmet

Batting helmets safeguard the back and sides of your head and often feature a **grill or face guard** for added protection. If your helmet takes a hard hit, replace it immediately, especially if you suspect a **concussion**.

Leg Guards (Pads)

These pads protect your legs from ball impacts. Despite their size, modern designs allow for easier running while offering robust protection with **side wings**, thick padding, and adjustable straps.

Batting Gloves

Hands are particularly vulnerable, so invest in gloves with **thick padding** for the fingers, knuckles, and palms. Gloves made from **leather or synthetic materials** also feature ventilation to keep hands cool.

Shoes

Specialized batting shoes with **spikes** provide traction and flexibility. Spikes may be metal, rubber, or a combination of both.

Additional Protection

Batters also wear **thigh guards**, **abdominal guards (box)**, **arm guards**, and **chest guards**, often made from strong materials like high-density foam or polycarbonate.

Wicketkeeping: Tools of the Trade

Despite wearing heavy protective gear for long stretches, wicketkeepers are remarkably agile and capable of dazzling athletic feats.

Wicketkeeping Gloves

These gloves, often resembling cartoonish hands, provide flexibility and comfort. Wicketkeepers also wear **inner gloves** for added protection.

Wicketkeeping Helmet

A dedicated helmet is essential, offering frontal protection and a lightweight grill for an **unobstructed view**. Avoid using your batting helmet for wicketkeeping.

Wicketkeeping Pads

Designed for **agility**, these pads are lighter and smaller than batting pads, allowing lateral movement while protecting against low-impact balls.

Guards

Like batters, wicketkeepers wear **thigh**, **abdominal**, and **chest guards** to stay protected from stray balls and swinging bats.

Bowling Equipment

Bowling Shoes

Not to be used at a bowling alley, cricket bowling shoes are designed for grip and stability during the delivery stride. These shoes vary based on whether the bowler finishes with their **left foot or right foot forward.** Features include:

- **Sliding Sole**: For the front foot of the bowler's dominant side.
- **Rubber Sole**: For the back foot, enhancing traction.
- **Spikes**: Typically metal, they prevent slipping on the delivery run-up.

Bowling shoes also offer **extra cushioning** to reduce joint strain during the intense delivery motion.

Protective Guards

Some bowlers wear **thigh guards** and **abdominal guards** to protect themselves from balls hit straight back at them.

Fielding Equipment

Fielding Shoes

Fielding shoes, equipped with **metal and rubber studs**, provide the traction needed for quick directional changes on grass.

Fielder's Helmet

Close-in fielders often wear helmets with face guards to shield themselves from hard-hit balls or edges.

Sun Hat/Cap and Sunglasses

Fielders frequently use **hats** or **caps** for sun protection and **sunglasses** to track balls in the air. When transitioning to bowling, they hand these items to the umpire for safekeeping.

Practice Fielding Gloves

While catches are made bare-handed in matches, fielders often use protective gloves during practice sessions.

Protective Gear

Close fielders may wear **shin guards**, **chest guards**, and **abdominal guards** for added safety.

Chapter Thirteen

Gambling

The **International Cricket Council (ICC)** implements stringent measures to safeguard the integrity of cricket. Its **anti-corruption unit** actively monitors the sport to detect and prevent match-fixing, investigating suspicious activities to ensure fair play.

Regardless of personal views on gambling, it has become an increasingly prominent aspect of the sports world, constituting a **multi-billion dollar industry.** Many popular betting apps—legal in certain U.S. states—offer cricket betting, including various types of live and prop bets.

Common Types of Cricket Bets

Match Betting

- **Match Winner**: Wager on which team will win the match.
- **Toss Winner**: Bet on the outcome of the coin toss before the match begins.

In-Play Betting

- **Next Wicket**: Predict which player will be the next to get out.
- **Next Over Runs:** Bet on how many runs will be scored in the next over.
- **Live Player Performance:** Wager on an individual player's performance during the match, such as runs scored or wickets taken.

Player Bets

- **Top Batter**: Predict which player will score the most runs in a match or series.

- **Top Bowler:** Bet on the player who will take the most wickets in a match or series.
- **Player of the Match:** Wager on the player who will be awarded the player of the match title.

Team Bets

- **Total Runs**: Predict the total number of runs scored by a team in a match.
- **Total Wickets:** Wager on the total number of wickets a team will take.
- **Highest Opening Partnership:** Bet on which team's opening pair will score the most runs.

Special Bets

- **Person of the Series**: Wager on the player awarded as the player of the series.
- **Century Scored:** Bet on whether a batter will score a century (100 runs) in a match.
- **Hat-Trick:** Predict whether a bowler will take three wickets in three consecutive deliveries.

Tournament Bets

- **Outright Winner**: Wager on which team will win the entire tournament.
- **Group Winner:** Bet on which team will top their group in a tournament.
- **Top Tournament Batter/Bowler:** Predict which player will score the most runs or take the most wickets in the tournament.

Glossary of Terms

Making Sense of Cricket Lingo

Terminology	Meaning
Aggregate	The total number of runs scored by a team or an individual in a series or season.
All Out	An innings that ends when the batting side runs out of batters.
All-rounder	A player skilled in both batting and bowling.
Appeal	A request made by a bowler or fielder to the umpire to dismiss the batter, typically expressed by shouting "howzat" or "howzee," or by simply turning to the umpire and cheering.
Bail	One of the two small pieces of wood that rest on top of the stumps to form the wicket.
Batter	The player attempting to hit the ball to score runs.
Batting Average	The average number of runs scored per innings by a batter, calculated by dividing the batter's total runs by the number of times they have been out.
Beamer	A ball that reaches the batter above waist height without bouncing.
Block	A defensive shot played to stop the ball safely without attempting to score runs.
Bouncer	A short, fast delivery that rises near the batter's head.
Boundary	A rope or other indicator marking the perimeter of the field. When the ball is hit to or over the edge of the field, it scores four or six runs.
Bowled	A dismissal of the batter that occurs when a delivery hits the stumps and removes at least one bail.

Terminology	Meaning
Bowler	The player currently delivering the ball to the batter. Unlike a baseball pitcher, a bowler must not bend their elbows during delivery.
Bowling Average	A statistic representing the number of runs conceded by a bowler divided by the number of wickets taken; a lower number is better.
Captain	A player who has been appointed as the leader of the team.
Catch	When a fielder catches the ball on the full (fly ball), resulting in the batter being out.
Caught	A dismissal in which a fielder catches the ball before it touches the ground.
Caught and Bowled	When the bowler catches the ball to dismiss the batter.
Centurion	A player who has scored a century.
Century	When a batter scores 100 runs in a single innings.
Check Upstairs	Invoking the Umpire Decision Review System (DRS) to the third umpire, usually seated high in the stadium.
Circle	A painted circle or ellipse centered in the middle of the pitch with a radius of 30 yards, marking where fielders can stand during one-day matches.
Come to the Crease	An expression for when the batter walks onto the playing field towards the crease to begin batting.
Crease	The lines marking the area where the batter stands.
Dead Ball	The state of play between deliveries during which batters may not score runs or be out. If the ball is not clearly dead, the umpire may signal that the ball is now dead.

Terminology	Meaning
Death Bowler	A bowler specializing in bowling during the challenging Death Overs at the end of a match. During Death Overs, batters play aggressively, and a good death bowler makes scoring runs difficult.
Death Overs	The final few overs of an innings in a limited overs match, during which batters try to score as many runs as possible.
Decision Review System (DRS)	The electronic system for reviewing calls, initiated by the umpire or a team captain.
Declaration	When a batting team voluntarily ends its innings before all players are out in Test cricket.
Delivery	The act of bowling the ball.
Dink	A deliberately gentle shot played with little power to guide the ball into an unguarded area of the field.
Direct Hit	When a fielder throws the ball directly at the wicket, resulting in an out without first being thrown to a fielder near the stumps, typically during a run-out attempt.
Dismissal	Getting a batter out, also referred to as a wicket.
Dot Ball	A delivery bowled without any runs being scored off it, recorded in the scorebook with a single dot.
Draw	A result in timed matches where the team batting last is not all out but fails to exceed their opponent's total.
Drinks	An agreed-upon short break in play during a session when refreshments are brought out to the players and umpires by the twelfth man on each side.
Duck	When a batter gets out without scoring any runs.

Terminology	Meaning
Duckworth-Lewis -Stern Method (DLS)	A method for determining a winner in a shortened match, typically due to bad weather. This formula calculates a revised target score for the team batting second based on the number of overs and wickets remaining.
Economical	A bowler who concedes very few runs in their over has a low economy rate.
End	The ground behind the stumps, designating from which end a bowler is bowling.
Expensive	A bowler who concedes a large number of runs in their overs has a high economy rate.
Extra	A run awarded to the batting team that is not credited to a specific batter. There are five types: byes, leg byes, wides, no-balls, and penalties. Wides and no-balls are recorded as runs for bowling analysis, but the others are not attributed to the bowler.
Fall	Refers to the dismissal of the batter.
Fast Bowler	A bowler who delivers the ball at high speeds.
Fence	The boundary.
Fielder	A player on the fielding side who is neither a bowler nor the wicketkeeper.
Find the Gap	To play a shot along the ground into the gaps between fielders.
Four	When the ball hits the ground before reaching the boundary, scoring four runs.
Free Hit	A penalty given in some forms of cricket when a bowler bowls a no-ball. The bowler must deliver another ball, and the batter cannot be dismissed by the bowler on that delivery.
Golden Duck	Getting out on the very first ball faced.
Googly	A leg-spin delivery that turns in the opposite direction to a normal leg break.

UNDERSTANDING CRICKET

Terminology	Meaning
Groundsman	The person responsible for maintaining the cricket field and preparing the pitch.
Half Century	A batter scoring 50 runs or more but fewer than 100. This is a significant achievement, and the number of half-centuries is tracked in player statistics.
Hat Trick	A bowler taking three consecutive wickets.
Hold Up an End	A batter intentionally restricting their scoring to concentrate on defense while their batting partner scores runs at the other end.
Hole Out	To be dismissed by being caught.
Hozat? or How's That?	A bowler or fielder asking the umpire to dismiss the batter, usually by shouting "howzat" or "howzee," or by simply turning to the umpire and cheering.
Hundred	• Century • 100-ball cricket • The Hundred tournament
Incoming Batter	The batter next in the batting order.
Innings	A period in which one team takes its turn to bat. Unlike baseball, in cricket, the term "innings" is both singular and plural.
Keeper	The player who stands behind the stumps to catch the ball; the wicketkeeper.
Knuckle Ball	A delivery where the fast bowler holds the ball on the knuckles of their index and middle fingers.
Laws of Cricket	Cricket has "laws" rather than rules. These laws are established by the Marylebone Cricket Club (MCC) and apply to cricket worldwide.
LBW (Leg Before Wicket)	A method of getting out if the ball hits the batter's leg and would have struck the stumps.
Length	The position along the pitch where the delivery bounces.

Terminology	Meaning
Limited Overs Match	A one-innings match, commonly referred to as one-day cricket.
Lolly	A ball that the batter can easily hit or that a fielder can easily catch.
Lord's Cricket Ground	Located in London and owned by the Marylebone Cricket Club (MCC), Lord's is often called the Mecca of Cricket or the Home of Cricket.
Lost Ball	A ball that cannot be retrieved due to being lost or out of reach. The umpire calls a dead ball to stop play, and a replacement ball is selected, preferably a used one in similar condition to the lost ball.
Lower Order	The batters who bat in positions 8-11 in the batting order.
Maiden Over	An over in which no runs are scored off the bat, and no wides or no-balls are bowled. Maiden overs are tracked as part of bowling analysis.
Marylebone Cricket Club (MCC)	The cricket club that owns the famous Lord's Cricket Ground in London and serves as the custodian of the laws of cricket. Lord's is often referred to as the Mecca of Cricket or the Home of Cricket.
Maximum	Equivalent to a Six; six runs.
Medium-pace	A bowler who delivers the ball slower than a pace bowler but faster than a spin bowler.
Middle Order	The batters who bat in positions 5-7 in the batting order. They are often all-rounders and include the wicketkeeper.
Misfield	A fielder who drops a catch or fumbles when attempting to pick up a ball.
Nervous Nineties	The period when a batter has a score between 90 and 99. Many batters feel anxious about getting out before reaching the century mark.

Terminology	Meaning
Net Run Rate (NRR)	The average run rate scored by a team minus the average run rate scored against them during a match. In a series, it is calculated as (total runs scored) / (total overs received) – (total runs conceded) / (total overs bowled). The NRR is often used as a tiebreaker in the group stage of tournaments.
New Ball	A new ball is used at the beginning of innings. In timed matches, the fielding captain has the option to take a new ball after 80 overs have been bowled. A new ball is harder and shinier than an old ball, moving faster through the air, which favors pace bowling, and it may swing after a few overs of polishing. In contrast, an old ball will be softer and rougher and will wear unevenly, favoring spin bowling.
No-ball	An illegal delivery by the bowler that gives the batter a free hit. The most common no-ball occurs when a bowler oversteps the popping crease with their foot.
No Man's Land	An area of the field where a fielder cannot save a single or stop a boundary.
No Result	The outcome of a limited overs match in which each team does not face the minimum number of overs required for a result, usually due to rain delays.
Non-striker	The batter standing at the bowling end.
Not Out	The umpire's decision when turning down an appeal for a wicket.
One Day International (ODI)	A limited overs match between two teams, consisting of two innings and capped at 50 overs per innings, played in a single day.

Terminology	Meaning
Opening Batter	One of the two batters who begin the innings. These batters often face the stronger bowlers and contend with the challenges of a shiny new ball. They also benefit from having fewer fielders in the outfield during the Powerplay.
Opening Bowler	One of the two bowlers who starts the innings with a new ball. They are typically the fastest or most aggressive bowlers, aiming to secure an early wicket. However, they face the challenge of having fewer fielders in the outfield during the Powerplay.
Out	A batter who has been dismissed. The umpire may call "out" while raising their index finger in response to an appeal for a wicket from the bowling side.
Over	A set of six legal deliveries bowled by a bowler.
Over Rate	The average number of overs bowled per hour.
Overthrows	Extra runs scored due to an errant throw from a fielder.
Pace/Fast Bowling	A bowling style characterized by deliveries at high speeds.
Par Score	During the second innings of a limited overs match, the par score is the target calculated by the Duckworth-Lewis-Stern method if the match were to be halted (e.g., due to rain). Updated after each ball, the par score helps assess whether the chasing team is ahead or behind the required run rate and wickets needed to win, which remains relevant even in uninterrupted matches.
Partnership	The combined runs scored by a pair of batters.

Terminology	Meaning
Picket Fences	A six-run over in which the score appears as "111111," resembling a picket fence.
Pink Ball	A ball used instead of a red ball, offering better visibility for day/night Test cricket matches .
Pitch	The rectangular area between the bowler and the batter, measuring 22 yards in length.
Popper	A ball that rises sharply after bouncing.
Popping Crease	One of the two lines in the field, located four feet in front of and parallel to the bowling crease, where the wickets are positioned. A batter who does not have either the bat or any part of their body touching the ground behind the popping crease is considered out of their ground and is at risk of being run out or stumped.
Powerplay	A block of overs (the first 6 in T20, the first 10 in ODI) that limits the number of fielders allowed in the outfield, giving a temporary advantage to the batting side.
Put Down	An expression indicating that a fielder has dropped a catch they should have made.
Quota	The maximum number of overs that may be bowled by each bowler (4 in T20, 10 in ODI).
Rabbit	A particularly poor batter, often an excellent bowler, who is expected to be dismissed cheaply almost every time. A "ferret" refers to a batter who is even worse than a rabbit.
Rain Delay	A halt in the game due to rain.
Rain Rule	A method, typically the Duckworth-Lewis-Stern method for determining the winner of a rain-shortened one-day match.
Red Ball	A ball dyed red, usually used in daytime Test matches.

Terminology	Meaning
Referral/Review	Requesting the third umpire to review a call using the Decision Review System.
Release	The moment in the bowling action when the bowler lets go of the ball.
Required Run Rate/Asking Rate	The run rate needed by the batting team to win in the second innings of a limited overs match. This is calculated as the number of runs required to beat the opposing team by one run divided by the number of overs remaining.
Reserve Day	A free day during a tournament available to make up for a match that has been washed out.
Result	The final outcome of a match, which can be a win, loss, draw, or tie. A no result can occur due to a washout or if a match is abandoned before it begins.
Retire	A batter who voluntarily leaves the field during their innings, usually due to injury or illness.
Review	A request for a DRS (Decision Review System) review in the hopes that the third umpire will overturn the on-field decision.
Rough	A worn-down section of the pitch, often from bowlers' footmarks, from which spinners can obtain more turn.
Run	The basic unit of scoring in cricket. The team with the most runs wins the match.
Run Chase	The team batting last trying to win the match by scoring more runs than the other team.
Run Out	A dismissal by a member of the fielding side who breaks the wicket while the batter is outside their crease making a run.
Run Rate/Runs Per Over (RPO)	The average number of runs scored per over.

UNDERSTANDING CRICKET

Terminology	Meaning
Safe	A batter is considered safe when they have grounded their bat or body in the popping crease before a fielder can break the wicket.
Seam	The raised stitching running around the circumference of the ball. It can also refer to the deviation of the ball after it bounces on its seam.
Seam Bowling	A bowling style that utilizes the raised seam or uneven wear of the ball to create deviation upon bouncing off the pitch.
Sent In	A team that loses the toss but bats first is said to have been sent in by the opposing captain.
Series	A set of matches in the same format played between the same two teams, often in different locations.
Session	A period of play divided into segments: from the start to lunch, from lunch to tea, and from tea to stumps.
Sight Screen	A large board positioned behind the bowler, beyond the boundary, to help the batter see the ball clearly. The board is typically white when a red ball is used and black when a white ball is used.
Signal	Body motions used by the umpire to indicate decisions to the players and the scorer.
Single	A run scored by the batters running only once between the wickets.
Sitter	A very easy catch.
Six	When the ball is hit over the boundary without touching the ground, scoring six runs.
Slog	A powerful shot in which the batter hits the ball high and long, aiming to reach the boundary.

Terminology	Meaning
Slower Ball	A medium-pace delivery bowled by a fast bowler to deceive the batter into playing the ball too early, resulting in a pop-up to a fielder.
Soft Hands (batting)	When the batter holds the bat loosely, allowing it to absorb the ball's momentum.
Spin Bowling	A style of bowling in which a spin bowler ("spinner") attempts to deceive the batter by imparting spin on the ball using either their fingers or wrist. Spin bowling is most effective when the ball travels relatively slowly, so most spinners bowl at a pace between 40 and 55 mph.
Spirit of Cricket	The concept of good conduct and sportsmanship.
Sticky Wicket	A difficult, wet pitch.
Strike Rate	A batting percentage calculated by dividing the number of runs scored by a batter by the number of balls faced. In bowling, it represents the average number of deliveries bowled before a bowler takes a wicket.
Striker	The batter who faces the active bowler.
Stump	One of the three vertical posts that make up the wicket.
Stumped	When the wicketkeeper breaks the wicket while the batter is out of their crease.
Substitute	A player who can replace another on the fielding side in case of illness or injury. The substitute is not allowed to bat, bowl, or keep wicket.
Super Over	A tiebreaking method used for tied T20 and ODI games, consisting of an extra over for each side. The team captains can choose any of their players to bat or bowl. The match ends if a second wicket is dismissed. After the Super Over for each side, the team with the most runs wins the match.

Terminology	Meaning
Swing Bowling	A bowling style typically used by fast and medium-pace bowlers. The fielding side polishes one side of the ball; as the innings continues, the ball becomes worn on one side while remaining shiny on the other. When bowled with the seam upright, the air travels faster over the shiny side than the worn side, causing the ball to swing (curve) in the air. Conventional swing means the ball curves away from the shiny side.
T20/Twenty20	A format in which each side has one innings of 20 overs.
Target	The score the batting team must achieve to win the match.
Test Cricket	A format that lasts up to five days and includes two innings for each team.
Third Umpire	An off-field umpire equipped with a television monitor to assist the on-field umpires.
Tie	The result of a cricket match in which the scores of both teams are equal, and the team batting last is all out; or, in a limited overs match, when the allotted overs have been completed. This should not be confused with a draw, where neither team wins, but the scores are not equal.
Top Order	The batters who bat in the top four positions of the batting order.
Toss	The flipping of a coin to determine which captain will have the right to choose between batting or fielding first.
Tour	An organized itinerary of matches that requires travel away from the team's usual base, particularly for the representative team of one nation playing a series of matches in another nation.

Terminology	Meaning
Turn	When a batter grounds the bat at the end of a run while changing direction to attempt another run.
Tweaker	An informal term for a spin bowler.
Two	A batter's call to attempt two runs, requiring their partner to commit to a quick turn.
Umpire	An official who enforces the laws of cricket and adjudicates play.
Umpire's Call	The outcome of the Decision Review System when the third umpire finds the evidence inconclusive. The original umpire's call stands, but the review does not count towards the team's limit on unsuccessful reviews.
Unbeaten Power Play	A situation where the batting team has not lost any wickets during the Power Play.
Wash Out	A match or day's play abandoned with little or no action due to rain.
White Ball	The ball typically used during T20 and day/night matches, as it is easier to see under artificial lighting.
Whites	The white clothing worn during Test cricket.
Wicket	Refers to the stumps and bails, and also an "out" in cricket.
Wicketkeeper	The player on the fielding side who stands behind the batter and is the only fielding player allowed to wear gloves.
Wickets In Hand	The number of wickets/outs remaining in the innings for the batting side.
Wide	A ball bowled too far from the batter, resulting in an extra run for the batting team.
Yorker	A delivery bowled to pitch at the base of the stumps or the batter's feet.

www.ingramcontent.com/pod-product-compliance
Lightning Source LLC
Chambersburg PA
CBHW071741120626
46550CB00002B/606